Praise for *Shakespeare Saved My Life*

"An uplifting, inspirational story of the strong connection between two unlikely friends, united by the power of books. Laura Bates shows the powerful effect of reaching out and touching someone else's life, no matter the circumstances. A must-read for anyone who has been changed by a book."

—Laura Schroff, *New York Times* bestselling co-author of *An Invisible Thread*

"I was really impacted by [*Shakespeare Saved My Life*]...I was so fascinated and touched by the growth of Larry (and his fellow classmates). And then that ending...I wanted to sit down and howl."

—Anne McMahon, Boswell Books, Milwaukee, WI

"An eye-opening study reiterating the perennial power of books, self-discipline, and the Bard of Avon."

—*Kirkus*

"Wonderful...well written, easy to follow, and hard to put down. My hope is that this book will make people understand that education can change lives."

—Sue Jones, Auntie's Bookstore, Spokane, WA

"A powerful testament to how Shakespeare continues to speak to contemporary readers in all sorts of circumstances."

—*Booklist*

"The work that Laura Bates has been doing for years with prison inmates and Shakespeare is of extraordinary importance. It has a kind of beauty and symmetry all its own."

—David Bevington, Shakespeare scholar, University of Chicago

SHAKESPEARE *Saved* MY LIFE

Ten Years in Solitary with the Bard

Laura Bates

Cover design by Vivian Ducas
Cover illustration by Shane Rebenschied

From Bates, L. "'To Know My Deed': Finding Salvation through Shakespeare." In *Performing New Lives: Prison Theater*, edited by J. Shailor, 33–48. London and Philadelphia: Jessica Kingsley Publishers, 2011. Reprinted with permission of Jessica Kingsley Publishers.

This book is a memoir. It reflects the author's present recollections of her experiences over a period of years. Some names and characteristics have been changed, some events have been compressed, and some dialogue has been re-created.

Published by Sourcebooks, Inc.
P.O. Box 4410, Naperville, Illinois 60567-4410
(630) 961-3900
Fax: (630) 961-2168
www.sourcebooks.com

Library of Congress Cataloguing-in-Publication data is on file with the publisher.

Printed and bound in the United States of America.
VP 10 9 8 7 6 5 4 3 2 1

This is a book about a prisoner in solitary confinement
...and how his life was changed by Shakespeare.
It is also about a Shakespeare professor
...and how her life was changed by the prisoner.
Welcome to a world that few ever enter,
a world in which both prisoner and professor spent ten years together,
learning, sharing, and growing through Shakespeare.

I've been down this week.
I was thinking maybe I'm a little homesick.
Home. To me, I think it's more an ideal than a place.
Around the people you love, that's home, that's what excites me the most.
The possibility of enjoying some of my life with the people I love.
'Cause it goes quick, don't it?
Life. Don't it go?
I mean, I'm only thirty. I'm not old.
But, you know, I've been in here since I was a kid.
It just goes so fast. Man! It just goes so fast.
And everybody overlooks enjoying it.
They just put themselves into so many prisons.

—Larry Newton

Foreword

The work that Laura Bates has been doing for years with prison inmates and Shakespeare is of extraordinary importance. It has a kind of beauty and symmetry all its own.

I have had the remarkable experience of being with her in small group discussions, first at Chicago's Cook County Jail in 1996 and more recently with her inmate students in the correctional facilities of the state of Indiana, most notably the maximum-security Wabash Valley. Few experiences are as lastingly and vividly etched on my consciousness.

At the Chicago lockup, security guards ushered me through at least four heavily locked gates that clanged shut as I passed through them. I then found myself in a sizable, windowless room with Laura as teacher and some eight or nine prison inmates, all of them African Americans in the age range of twenty to thirty-five and guilty of violent crimes including homicide as students. But no armed guards were present. The business of the day was to work on what one might call the "rumble" scene, right at the center of *Romeo and Juliet*, when first Mercutio and then Tybalt are slain in street fighting. Laura took her students through the scene, word by word, making sure that everyone understood what was being said. This led to a discussion of the ethics of gang warfare, hearkening back to the opening scene of the play with its violent confrontation of Capulets versus Montagues. Who started the brawl in act 3, scene 1? Who or what was to blame for the ancient quarrel between the two families? Why does Mercutio challenge Tybalt to a fight? What are we to make of the gentle words Romeo has for Tybalt when Romeo has been openly insulted by his opposite number? What do Romeo's friends make of his "calm, dishonorable, vile submission"? Is Romeo to blame for changing his mind after the death of Mercutio? To what extent are peer pressures responsible for his decision to fight Tybalt? On all these matters, the student inmates called on their own extensive experience with gang rivalries and machismo codes of male honor. Everything they said seemed beautifully appropriate to me.

Then Laura had them stand up and speak their lines as dialogue. They did quite well, even if the proper names came across as strange: Tybalt, Mercutio, Capulet, and Montague. Laura's next move was wonderful, I thought: she asked them to paraphrase what the lines said in their own habits of speech. "Hey, man, let's get out of here," said Benvolio to Mercutio. "It's hot, man, and those dudes the Capulets will be here any minute and there's going to be trouble." "You have about as much courage as a sick chicken," said Mercutio in reply. "If you don't have a couple of drinks in you, your face turns as white as my shirt." And so it went, with greater and lesser degrees of accuracy. Laura was cool. She was in charge. She didn't stand for any nonsense, but she listened, she helped, she respected. The men were plainly willing to be doing what they were doing. A gutsy performance on all sides.

Years later, I visited Laura at Indiana State University, where I had the stirring experience of talking with some of Laura's student inmates in the Indiana correctional system. They asked good questions. They talked with one another. The subject at hand was *Macbeth*. Even gutsier than her *Romeo and Juliet* work in Chicago is her work with *Macbeth* in solitary confinement.

Recently, I copresented with Laura at a Shakespeare conference, where she showed a documentary of her work at the Wabash Valley Correctional Facility. Here the prisoners were not only inmates of Indiana's maximum-security prison, but they were also in solitary confinement because they were judged to be especially violent and thus dangerous to guards and other inmates alike. They were in individual cells, each with a small aperture at waist height designed to facilitate the passing into the cell of food or whatever. Their voices could be heard, and their faces were partly visible when they crouched down at the aperture. They were escorted from their cells one at a time with two armed guards. No other person was allowed in the corridor when a prisoner was released into that space. Here it was that Laura sat on an improvised chair, asking questions, leading a discussion about Macbeth's decision to kill Banquo. It is terrific that these prisoners have a chance to read and think about *Macbeth*, because what hangs over the play so much is the sense of fallen human nature and the threat of temptation that even an honorable man cannot resist: there but for the grace of God go I.

The most remarkable of all the inmates whom I've gotten to know through Laura at the Wabash Valley Correctional Facility is Larry Newton, the subject of this fine book. Laura set up an interview between Larry and me one day. I was impressed at once with Larry: a serious person, gracious, good-humored, alive with intellectual curiosity. Laura suggested to Larry that he start things off by asking me questions that were on his mind.

Larry asked me, "Do you think that Shakespeare wrote *King John* after the death of his own child? The pain he describes just seems so real."

To say the least, this question took me entirely by surprise.

Larry was raising one of the most sophisticated and detailed questions in Shakespearean scholarship today. Stephen Greenblatt, in his *Will in the World*, has weighed in on the side of arguing that *King John* needs to come after the death of Shakespeare's only son at the age of eleven, because Constance's exquisite lament for the plight of her son Geoffrey ("Grief fills the room up of my absent child," etc., 3.4.93) reads like a personal response on Shakespeare's part to an unbearable loss. I am skeptical because we find other equally moving tributes to the death of a son in earlier plays, like Lord Talbot's sad tribute to his slain son and heir young John Talbot in *Henry the Sixth, Part One*, 4.7.1–16 ("and there died / My Icarus, my blossom, in his pride"). And there are others. *King John* seems earlier than 1595–6, when Shakespeare wrote *Richard the Second*.

The point here is not my attempt at an answer, but the remarkably probing and well-informed nature of the question. Larry had clearly done a lot of reading, all the more remarkable considering he did not have access to books about Shakespeare, getting his insights instead from the Shakespearean texts themselves. We talked about the death of Shakespeare's son Hamnet and the dating of *King John*, and moved on to other matters, prompted again by his intellectual curiosity. Our conversation lasted over an hour and touched on at least ten plays. Clearly, Larry was not just throwing me preplanned, researched questions. I was amazed.

He says that he wants to be the first prisoner in the state of Indiana to earn a PhD while incarcerated. I have no doubts of his ability.

David Bevington
University of Chicago

Chapter 1

Favorite Freakin' Shakespeare

"Oh, man, this is my favorite freakin' quote!"

What professor wouldn't like to hear a student enthuse so much over a Shakespeare play—a Shakespeare *history* play, no less! And then to be able to flip open the two-thousand-page *Complete Works of Shakespeare* and find the quote immediately: "When that this body did contain a spirit, a kingdom for it was too small a bound"!

He smacks the book as he finishes reading. Meanwhile, I'm still scrambling to find the quote somewhere in *Henry the Fourth, Part One*.

"Act uh…?"

"Act 5, scene 4," my student informs me, again smacking the page with his enthusiastic fist. "Oh, man, that is *crazy*!"

Yes, *this* is crazy: I am sitting side-by-side with a prisoner who has just recently been allowed to join the general prison population after more than ten years in solitary confinement. We met three years prior, in 2003, when I created the first-ever Shakespeare program in a solitary confinement unit, and we spent three years working together in that unit. Now we have received unprecedented permission to work together, alone, unsupervised, to create a series of Shakespeare workbooks for prisoners. Newton is gesticulating so animatedly that it draws the attention of an officer walking by our little classroom. He pops his head inside.

"Everything okay in here?" he asks.

"Just reading Shakespeare," I reply.

He shakes his head and walks on.

"That is *crazy*!" Newton repeats, his head still in the book.

A record ten and a half consecutive years in solitary confinement, and he's not crazy, he's not dangerous—he's reading Shakespeare.

And maybe, just maybe, it is *because* he's reading Shakespeare that he is not crazy, or dangerous.

Chapter 2

The Value of Education

O*stracized*. When I was a kid growing up in the 1960s in a west side Chicago ghetto, I didn't know what the word meant. I didn't know what many words meant because my immigrant parents didn't speak English. With both a linguistic and a cultural gap, I often felt out of place among my classmates at the public school. I felt, well, ostracized.

As World War II refugees from Eastern Europe, my parents had lost everything: home, possessions, friends, and family. Although they could not teach my sister and me the English language, they taught us a far more important lesson: the value of education. "No one can ever take that from you," my mother told us. She had never had the chance to attain an education herself beyond six years of elementary school. One of four children raised on a little farm in the "old country," her parents could afford to educate only every other child... and she was the other. Her older brother became a carpenter's apprentice, and her sister went to nursing school. But she and her younger brother stayed home to help herd the sheep and harvest potatoes.

The war came and shattered lives. Years later, this uneducated young woman found herself in the big city in a foreign country halfway around the world. At the age of twenty-three, she had married her childhood sweetheart the day before fleeing their homeland. They had expected to share the rough journey together, but on boarding the refugee train, the men were separated from the women. My mother spent the next five years searching for her husband, her brothers, or any living relative. She never found any, so eventually she traveled to America—alone. Ten stormy days crossing the ocean: in Shakespeare's words, "tempest-tossed."

Although my mother must have been terrified many times, my favorite recollections are of her spunk (like the time she refused to give up her purse to a would-be mugger). Not surprisingly, I inherited her mix of fearlessness and fearfulness. The dangerous ghetto environment I grew up in did not scare me, but bridges, elevators, even cars did. A thunderstorm would have me running into the basement, and any insect would have me running out of the house. I walked the dark streets alone at night but could not sleep without the reassuring sound of a little black-and-white TV—to the chagrin of my sister, with whom I shared a bedroom. My list of personal phobias was quite long. At the top of the list, inspired by my mother's terrifying ocean journey, was boats.

Twenty years later, at the age of twenty-five, when I first entered a prison, I was less frightened by the convicts staring at me behind the bars of their cells than I was by the rickety elevator that took me to my basement classroom. I started doing volunteer work in Chicago's Cook County Jail because of an argument with my husband's friend, John Bergman, a theater practitioner working in maximum-security prisons. "Those guys are beyond rehabilitation," I insisted. "You should focus on first-time offenders." And, to test my own hypothesis, that's what I did. At the time, I could not have imagined that eventually I would be working in *super*max—that is, the long-term solitary confinement unit, the prison within the prison.

In prison, I was again fearless in an environment where most people would be fearful, and maybe that is why I was able to successfully reach those prisoners when others could not. I also recalled my mother's words about education. Like war refugees, prisoners have lost everything: home, possessions, friends, and often family. For a prisoner, education has a special value as the one thing that no one can take from him.

When I began my journey into prison in 1983, I tutored first-time offenders in a basic literacy program through the PACE Institute at Chicago's Cook County Jail. (PACE is an acronym for Programmed Activities in Correctional Education.) I discovered that some of the prisoners I worked with were from my old neighborhood. And, in a strange way, I felt at home.

I felt much less comfortable when, ten years later, I went back to school to finish the college education I had discontinued to take on a full-time job. My goal was to complete that bachelor's degree so I could continue on toward a PhD—making up for my mother's lack of education in an incongruous way.

While negotiating the unfamiliar terrain of academia and grappling with unfamiliar concepts such as literary theory, I once again returned to the more familiar ground of prison in 1993. This time, I was inspired by a comment made in a lecture by a famous literary scholar, who asserted that Shakespeare's play *Macbeth* represented "the ipso facto valorization of transgression." He seemed to be suggesting that Macbeth's acts of transgression (murder) were worthy of praise, but I couldn't help feeling that real-life transgressors would disagree, that they would feel that "valorization" of transgression was anything but "ipso facto"! And that conviction would eventually lead me to work with Shakespeare in prison.

With a graduate degree in hand, I started working as a college instructor in prison, teaching introductory-level English classes to incarcerated students pursuing an undergraduate degree in several medium- and maximum-security facilities in Indiana. Some years later, I would make my way into supermax: the long-term solitary confinement unit housing the state's most dangerous prisoners.

My sister, the levelheaded and responsible one, cautioned me.

"What do you think," I replied with a laugh, "that I'll be taken hostage?"

I can laugh about it now, but the very first time I stepped into supermax, I really could have been.

Chapter 3

Breaking Out

One warm spring day in May of 2000, a short but stocky Caucasian prisoner named Newton was playing an innocent-looking game of basketball with three other prisoners on a little concrete-enclosed recreation pad at Wabash Valley Correctional Facility. Each time he reached up to make a shot, his arms revealed an assortment of tattoos. He was younger than the other prisoners, only in his mid-twenties, but he'd spent nearly a decade in prison already, much of it in solitary confinement. In those days, prisoners in the Wabash Valley solitary confinement unit were allowed to have group recreation, but all that would change because of the events about to unfold. Afterward, there would be no group recreation. There wouldn't even be a basketball.

Suddenly, on cue, one of the prisoners fell to the ground, clutching his ankle. The other three rushed to the door, banging on it, shouting in unison: "Nurse! Hey, we need a nurse back here!" The plan called for a hostage with whom to negotiate. Not necessarily a release to the streets; they knew that wasn't going to happen. But some of the prisoners thought they could negotiate for better living conditions. Newton just wanted to cause enough mayhem to get shipped out of the Wabash Valley supermax, even if it was only to another supermax.

They kept calling: "Hey! Need a *nurse*!"

Newton turned to the prisoner on the ground: "Moan or something, man!"

"Ohhh! Ohhhh!" The man faked a moan, but it wasn't convincing enough. Instead of a nurse, they got four armed officers. Newton watched them approach, feeling himself get hot and angry. It was a familiar feeling. It didn't take much; he was always angry in those days.

Now he turned to his partners and shrieked. "What? Like they think they can just come in here and punk us off the rec pad?!"

He shoved one of them toward the steel door. "Open the door!"

"Huh?"

"I said, open the freakin' door!" (Newton didn't like to cuss, even among his peers.)

The man was frozen. Newton pushed him aside. "Forget it. I'll do it!" With some difficulty, he managed to slide open the door, which he had secretly set from locking with some batteries when the group had been brought in. Facing the officers now, he was completely fearless—or, at least, he appeared to be.

"So what? You gonna *punk* us off the freakin' rec pad?!" He assumed a fighting stance, his weapon—a homemade knife—drawn. "Well, all right, come on then!"

The biggest, baddest officer was the first one on the cellhouse range and the first one off. Seeing the weapon in the hands of a prisoner with an extensive and violent history, he turned and fled. His partners started to spray Newton with OC (oleoresin capsicum, a high-intensity pepper spray). Newton grabbed one of the officers, Sgt. Harper, and started beating him in the face with some other batteries that he had placed in a sock. A tug-of-war ensued as the other officers tried to pull the sergeant away. In desperation, Newton took out his knife and stabbed the sergeant once in the shoulder.

By now, the spray had disoriented Newton to the point that the other officers were able to pull Harper out, roll the door closed, and seal off the range. The four prisoners were left in the range while the officers assembled their extraction team. With a lull in the action, a hush fell over the stunned prisoners who had been watching, glued to their cell doors. Feeling his way down the range, Newton stumbled from one cell door to the next. There are twelve side-by-side cells (six on the ground level and six upstairs) on each range in the solitary confinement unit, each with a little slot in the steel door that the prisoners have to put their hands through to be handcuffed prior to leaving their cells. These cuff ports are usually kept locked, but Newton, working his way from the recreation pad that was located at the end of the range, finally found one that was open.

"Hey, man," he begged the invisible prisoner inside the cell, "gimme some water, would you? I'm so blasted, I can hardly see!"

Instantly, another prisoner started shouting, "Hey! Hey! Call a medic! You fuckers blinded him!"

"Oh, man," Newton thought. "Like I need this!" The sink water was slow in coming; water pressure was minimal in this unit.

"Hey, man," said Newton after impatiently listening to the drip of the faucet. "Just flush the toilet and dip it out of there."

As he stood in the middle of the range pouring toilet water over his face, one of his useless partners approached and asked, "What do we do now?"

Newton just laughed. "Nothing. It's over with. We lost. I'm going in the shower, that's where I'm going." He made his way to the shower, wondering where he would be shipped next.

In May 2000, Newton was trying to break out of supermax, while I was trying to break in. Years later, when he related this episode to me, it occurred to me that our paths had nearly crossed back then.

"Your hostage could've been me," I said.

"That's true," he admitted. "We were so desperate back then, it could've been like: 'Whoever we can get, yeah!' Yeah," he added thoughtfully. He fell uncharacteristically silent for a minute. Then he said, "*Man!*"

"What?"

"I'm just so glad it wasn't."

"Yeah," I replied. "Me too."

Chapter 4

Breaking In

In May 2000, I was working as a part-time instructor in the Department of English at Indiana State University. I had just completed a PhD at the prestigious University of Chicago, working with one of the world's leading Shakespeare scholars, Professor David Bevington. And now I was teaching four composition courses a day to freshmen who couldn't care less about comma splices and sentence fragments. But on Friday nights, while my colleagues kicked back with a beer or two, I taught two additional courses in English literature to maximum-security prisoners, most of whom were genuinely hungry for knowledge and guidance to become better people. These classes took place at Wabash Valley Correctional Facility in downstate Indiana, in a facility that housed more than two thousand prisoners—the worst of these housed in the long-term disciplinary segregation Secured Housing Unit known as the SHU.

Critics of correctional education say that prisoners are motivated only by the time cut. (In some states, they can reduce their sentence by a year or two by earning a degree.) I have two responses to that. One: Why is a prisoner's motivation to earn a degree so that he can return to his family sooner viewed more negatively than a campus student's motivation to earn a degree so he can make more money? And, two: What about the motivation of a prisoner, like Newton, who is serving a sentence of life with no possibility of parole?

I had another lifer in my spring 2000 semester. Donald was a quiet loner who sat in the back of the room and rarely spoke. It wasn't until a couple of weeks before the end of the semester that I finally saw his missing teeth as he smiled. He came up to me after class and told me that our last reading assignment was really speaking to him.

The classes I taught as an adjunct instructor were introductory level. The class Donald attended was Introduction to American Literature, but I found a way to insert a little Shakespeare in every class I taught. Not only was Shakespeare my area of academic training, but I also felt strongly that these four-hundred-year-old works could offer contemporary students—and prisoners in particular—fresh insights into their own lives.

Our final reading assignment was *The Tragedy of Macbeth*. It's been a special piece of literature for me ever since I first read it at the age of ten. Well, I can't really say that I "read" it at that age, but I did check it out of my elementary school library. And I can still recall the thrill of poring over its archaic words that I knew meant something significant, that I hoped would someday mean something to me. By the time I reached high school, I was able to begin to make meaning out of the language. But it wasn't until I started teaching these plays, in prison, that their full meaning would come through: beautifully crafted works of literature written hundreds of years ago that can connect with us here and now.

The play *Macbeth*, for example, deals with a range of human emotions through the perspective of a good man who is considering doing what he knows is a bad deed: killing the king in order to become king. I was pleased that it was speaking to a student who had never spoken before.

But the following week, I learned that Donald had tried to

kill another prisoner and had been sent to the SHU. He was automatically withdrawn from college, as prisoners in the SHU were not permitted to be enrolled in college-credit courses. This was the end of Donald's education but the beginning of my own. It was the first time I had heard of the SHU, aka "supermax." I knew nothing about this other world of hard-core incarceration. My students informed me of the details.

"You're locked down all the time."

"No movement, none."

"No programming."

"Not even school."

"It's worse than death row," added Phil, who had done three years on the row.

Walking across the prison yard that evening with another instructor, I told my colleague what I had learned in class. He pointed at a windowless brick building in the distance. "That's the SHU," he said. And then, as if reading my mind, he added, "But a teacher could never get in there."

Breaking into the state's most secured unit would prove to be almost as difficult as breaking out. Neither one could be done legally.

I am not a hard-core criminal, but I have been known to occasionally bend the rules.

For example, there was the time I made a "house call" to pick up a homework assignment from a delinquent prisoner-student and then asked him to invite me into his cell. The prisoner looked at the officer on duty; the officer shrugged. I entered the cell.

"What about you?" I said to my student's cell mate. The startled prisoner was lying on his bunk in his underwear, watching a basketball game on his little black-and-white TV.

"Ma'am?" he said, pulling his sheet up to his waist and trying to process the idea of a *visitor* in his cell.

"Are you in college too?"

"Uh, no."

"Why not? What's your problem?"

"You must scare them," said my department chairperson at the university when I related the incident to him. *Me*...scare *them*? As a middle-aged Shakespeare professor, I'm hardly an intimidating presence. But maybe I did need to convince myself that I was fearless. Maybe that was one of my reasons for teaching in prison.

And maybe that's why I asked a friend—a prison administrator who used to work in the SHU—to take me in there for a little tour. I wanted to see the unit, and I wanted to see if I would be scared. I walked close beside her as we made our way through a series of locked gates and labyrinthine corridors. I took a deep breath and summoned the courage to stand alone in front of the glass pod from which an officer controlled the range doors and call out to the officer above: "Open Range One!" He did so because, well, how could anyone without authority to give such an order arrive into this netherworld?

The door rolled open, and I entered.

Chapter 5
I'm In

"Now I *know* you're crazy!"

That was the response of my department chairperson when, three years after my initial unofficial foray into the SHU, I burst into his office with the exciting news: "I just got permission to start a Shakespeare program in *solitary confinement*!"

At this point, I was a tenure-track assistant professor, teaching Shakespeare courses on campus and in prison through Indiana State University's Correction Education Program. After many years of teaching college-credit courses in several Indiana prisons, I had earned such a strong reputation that the superintendent of Wabash Valley Correctional Facility, which housed the solitary confinement unit, opened this unprecedented door. I thought that my new program in supermax would not only be valuable to these prisoners, but would also provide material for an article to help me to earn tenure and a permanent position at the university.

Unfortunately, like almost everyone else I knew, my boss was not very supportive of my work in prison. He worried about my safety, and he also resented the hours that it took away from my day job. He even tried to make it a condition of my employment that I teach on campus only, and reluctantly I agreed to "retire" from my teaching of college courses in prison. That lasted just one year, and then the director of Volunteer Services at the prison asked me to begin a voluntary program for prisoners, adding, "I think we could get you into the SHU as well."

"I don't want to shut any doors," I told my boss, who was shaking his head at my foolhardiness. "And whatever door they open, I'll go through."

"You're crazy," he repeated as I left his office.

One friend openly admitted, "I think they should all be making license plates. They don't deserve education." But I wasn't sure that I thought of education as a treat. Nor did I think of it as punishment either, as another friend said to me, "Don't make them read Shakespeare; they're already in prison!"

What did I think? Why did I want to enter solitary confinement? Certainly, there was the challenge, and I have always relished a challenge. Just being told "you can never get in there" was enough to make me want to get in there. I was also curious about the people in this most extreme form of incarceration: Were they really so dangerous? Were they all insane? Or had we silenced voices that needed to be heard? Finally, I was curious to see what this other world was like. I had done a bit of traveling in my life, and I was certain that this would be like no place on Earth.

I was right.

Those were the reasons that I wanted to enter this extreme environment, but I was less clear on why I wanted to *work* there: to volunteer my free time every week; to drive two hours, round-trip, after a full day of teaching on campus; to enter through so many razor-wire fences and steel doors; to face the most dangerous prisoners in the state; to ask them to read Shakespeare? What in the world did I get myself into? These were some of the thoughts bouncing through my mind as I drove home that day.

My favorite Dave Matthews song came on the radio. "I will go in this way / and find my own way out," Dave sang. Whatever might happen, I figured I would find my own way too.

Chapter 6

Newton's In

DOC number 91-43-82: Life. Assault history. Escape history. Possession of dangerous weapons. Tampering with locks. Attempted escape. Escape. Group demonstration. Battery. Battery with a weapon. Battery on an officer."

The casework manager put down the document and looked at me. Everyone in the room, prison administrators and corrections officers, looked at me. She had just read the conduct history of one of the prisoners I had requested for my first Shakespeare group. I figured I was in trouble.

With a cheery voice, I said the only thing I could think of: "Is there any reason I can't work with him?"

They weren't expecting that, so they didn't have an answer. They looked at one another. The casework manager spoke: "I guess not. But we just want you to know what you're in for."

I had no idea.

In the twenty years I had spent working as a volunteer and as an instructor in minimum- and maximum-security prisons in Chicago and in Indiana, I had never met an inmate who scared me—until Newton. I had never rejected one—until Newton. The day we met, I was going cell to cell in the SHU looking for prisoners interested in reading Shakespeare. Eventually, I would have as many as fifty prisoners on my waiting list, nearly one out of every four housed in the unit. At the beginning, I would have been happy to find at least one. But when I looked at Newton through the pegboard steel door of his cell, I was struck by the quiet intensity of this caged beast and crossed his name off of my list, thinking, "I can't work with this one."

So what was I doing one week later, fighting for special permission to get one of the allegedly most dangerous prisoners in the state's supermax unit into my Shakespeare program? Was it the "challenge" thing again? No. It wasn't something in me; it was something in Newton. And it was obvious from the start—not the first time he looked at me or the first time he spoke to me, but the first time he wrote for me. It was in response to the initial Shakespeare assignment I distributed to segregated prisoners to screen prospective participants: a soliloquy from the last act of Shakespeare's history play *Richard the Second*.

Spoken by the overthrown king who is now imprisoned, the speech begins: "I have been studying how I may compare this prison where I live unto the world: and for because the world is populous and here is not a creature but myself, I cannot do it." Along with the speech, I attached a blank sheet of paper with one question: *What do you understand from the excerpt?*

While most prisoners scribbled a brief response, Newton submitted a full page, both sides, with incongruous smiley faces punctuating every few sentences:

> *I understand that he is in prison, and clearly in a type of solitary confinement.* ☺ *His thoughts are his only companions, his method for populating this empty world so that it can be compared to the world outside of those walls. He had studied a way to compare the two—so it is clearly his attempt. I cannot tell if it is extremely complex or rather simple? It seems like you can spend time on just about each passage and come up with three different conclusions.*

That comment alone earned him a place in the program. Awareness of multiplicity of interpretation is the key to reading Shakespeare. And then Newton continued with a college-level example of close critical reading and explication of a literary passage:

> *Like in the area dedicated to scripture. It appears as though he is a believer in the word as it is the "better sort" and having so much time to think, no thought is "contented" as he says, and the better thoughts are exposing flaws or contradictions. Making him doubt, at least challenging him to doubt. If so, it must be a scary idea to lose the "better sort" of thought.* ☺
>
> *I struggle to bring out the comparisons, because to me it only speaks of his conduct in there. His thoughts, conclusions, and he seems to be making a statement rather than a comparison. I can relate to much of it, if I am right in reading it, or maybe it is art left for interpretation?*

Not bad for a fifth-grade dropout. What came next was a prisoner's perspective on the passage, exactly the kind of insight I looked for in my prison work:

> *I can really relate to the thoughts of ambition plotting unlikely wonders!* ☺ *I can see him now pacing around and playing out these great fantasies and then the quick reality check and it leaves and he feels silly. Maybe that is what he meant by "die in their own pride"?*

And his conclusion captured the deeper philosophical lesson about the meaning of life in Richard's speech:

> *I guess as in art, I can overcomplicate the work, so I will just close it up. It seems to me that he has gone from king to prisoner, and in his thoughts goes back and forth, but seems to conclude with*

saying that until you have been at peace, or content, with nothing...you cannot be pleased with anything. Or that you cannot be truly happy until you have come to terms with being nothing. ☺

Wow. That was the most thoughtful response I had ever gotten to an initial Shakespeare assignment—in prison or on campus. And Newton didn't even know who Shakespeare was.

Chapter 7
Life Inside

So what's it like in there?

The supermax unit that housed Newton when we met in 2003 is a different place today since a recent Human Rights Watch lawsuit found the conditions to be inhumane. Back then, it was dirty: floors were littered with tossed food trays and homemade "parachutes" or "kites" (messages tied to strings that are sent across the range floor) and other contraband. It was noisy: tormented cries of the criminally insane and shouted taunts of hostile prisoners filled the ranges. It was smelly: overflowing toilets, remnants of food trays, and human body odor created a stench. Hot in summer. Cold in winter.

The individual windowless concrete cells contained a concrete bunk bed with a thin mattress, a stainless-steel platform and bench that served as a table and chair, plus a toilet and sink. The metal pegboard door obscured the view to the other side, but there was nothing on the other side except another concrete wall. Inmates were housed in side-by-side cells, so there was no face-to-face view of another human being—except when an officer shoved a food tray into the slot or when the nurse delivered a pill. In the SHU, there were 288 such cells (twelve on each range), in which isolated prisoners spent nearly twenty-four hours a day with no human contact—for months, even years at a time. In Newton's case, it was a record ten years.

Think of all you've done over the past ten years: gotten a degree, gotten married, had a baby? Or maybe just gotten a new kitten or puppy? Newton had done none of that.

Think of all the places you've seen: a city skyline, a mountain landscape, a beach at sunset? Newton had seen none of that.

Now think of all the choices you make every day: what to wear, what to have for dinner, whom to call on the phone—these are choices Newton had not made in more than a decade.

Think of simply stopping at a stoplight, deciding which way to go. Are you going to go forward or turn? Either road leads someplace. "Man," said Newton. "That's freedom!"

During my SHU orientation days, I walked the ranges accompanied by Father Bob, the resident chaplain. With his long gray ponytail, his denim attire, and his laid-back demeanor, he reminded me of Willie Nelson (one of my husband's favorite singers). "Hey, Father!" an inmate called out to him one day. "My brother's dying. Would you pray with me?" I stepped back to offer a little privacy in this unit that offered none, and from across the range, I saw Father Bob's head bent in prayer next to the inmate's, the steel cell door between them like the partition of a confessional stand.

No volunteer had ever worked in this unit before, so there was no volunteer training program in place. Instead, I was required to complete the standard weeklong training program along with officers and other prison staff. I learned:

- How to respond in a hostage situation
- How to perform CPR
- How to handle hazardous waste
- How to frisk and handcuff an offender
- How to throw off an attacker (when I got home that

evening, I practiced this move on my husband, a former college wrestling coach—and it worked!)

The following week, I walked the ranges unescorted, ever mindful of Father Bob's caveat: "Be ready for anything. Every time you step out onto a range, it's different." That's true; there was no such thing as a routine day in the SHU. I quickly learned that it wasn't the noisy ranges but the quiet ones—eerily quiet—that I needed to worry about. Whenever I stepped onto a quiet range, I wondered whether everyone was sleeping, or medicated, or planning the next prison riot.

As soon as the steel gate that sealed off each range of twelve cells was rolled open—through remote control by an officer in the glass pod above—the prisoners on the lower level alerted those upstairs: "Female on the range!" I received a variety of greetings, as you might expect. Immediately, some of them got an urge to pee, sidling up to the toilet at the front of their cell, barely visible through the steel pegboard cell door. In the beginning they assumed that I was a visiting psychologist or a new counselor. Volunteers never entered the SHU. Once they got to know me, they called out, "Shakespeare on the range!"

The officers informed me that being "gunned down" was the biggest risk—not with bullets, but with semen, urine, or worse. So I started to keep a change of clothes in the car, just in case. The floors were often wet, with God knows what, so I also designated a special pair of SHU shoes.

Because of Newton's stabbing of Sgt. Harper (the only stabbing incident in the history of the SHU), the central administration in Indianapolis issued a mandate that everyone who worked in the SHU—officers, counselors, and, yes, even the Shakespeare professor—wear a bulletproof (i.e., knife-proof) vest. It was bulky and weighed a ton. One day, I dropped my pen on the floor and couldn't even bend over to pick it up. The officers complained: "If we fall over in them things, we're like a turtle on his back. Fuckin' dumbasses in Central Office!" (In my experience, male officers often cussed in the presence of a female visitor; prisoners rarely did so, and when they did, they usually apologized.)

I soon learned that the most popular reading material among SHU inmates was true-crime stories. Typical topics for conversation on the ranges were pro wrestling, hot rods, hot women the inmates have known, and what they'd like to do to the officers.

"You'll never get these guys to talk about Shakespeare," an inmate told me.

Chapter 8

The First Lesson I Teach

I have been studying how I may compare
This prison where I live unto the world:
And for because the world is populous
And here is not a creature but myself,
I cannot do it; yet I'll hammer it out.
My brain I'll prove the female to my soul,
My soul the father; and these two beget
A generation of still-breeding thoughts,
And these same thoughts people this little world,
In humours like the people of this world,
For no thought is contented. The better sort,
As thoughts of things divine, are intermix'd
With scruples and do set the word itself
Against the word:
As thus, 'Come, little ones,' and then again,
'It is as hard to come as for a camel
To thread the postern of a small needle's eye.'
Thoughts tending to ambition, they do plot
Unlikely wonders; how these vain weak nails
May tear a passage through the flinty ribs
Of this hard world, my ragged prison walls,
And, for they cannot, die in their own pride.

Thoughts tending to content flatter themselves
That they are not the first of fortune's slaves,
Nor shall not be the last; like silly beggars
Who sitting in the stocks refuge their shame,
That many have and others must sit there;
And in this thought they find a kind of ease,
Bearing their own misfortunes on the back
Of such as have before endured the like.
Thus play I in one person many people,
And none contented: sometimes am I king;
Then treasons make me wish myself a beggar,
And so I am: then crushing penury
Persuades me I was better when a king;
Then am I king'd again: and by and by
Think that I am unking'd by Bolingbroke,
And straight am nothing: but whate'er I be,
Nor I nor any man that but man is
With nothing shall be pleased, till he be eased
With being nothing.

King Richard the Second, act 5, scene 5

This was the first lesson I taught in the SHU, following up on the initial assignment. I chose this excerpt to introduce segregated prisoners to Shakespeare because Richard is speaking from solitary confinement. I assumed that the prisoners would be able to relate. The day would include a group session in the specially designated wing where the prisoners would be brought and placed into individual cells, with me seated in the middle. But first, I had an individual session with Newton. He was not allowed to join the group. Given his history, he was considered to be too great of an escape risk. No doubt, the officers would not want to grant this offender anything that might seem like a privilege, either. But I was given permission to work with him at his cell each week.

Because I was working alone on this, my first day of actually teaching in the SHU, I had to figure out how to get my handouts through the closed cuff port in the middle of the cell door by myself. Surely, the inmate inside was not going to be able to help me. With some difficulty, I managed to slide the stiff metal bar, pull down the little ledge, and place the sheet of paper on the opened cuff port.

"Mr. Newton!" I called out into the darkness of the cell, wondering whether he was awake or asleep...or something else.

"Mr. Newton?" Momentarily, I saw a shadowy figure approach the door, and from inside the cell, a hand reached out to receive the paper. It was slender, almost delicate, pale white from years without sun exposure, and adorned with tattoos. The pegboard door allowed only 60 percent visibility, so my first glimpses of Newton were not very revealing. I could tell only that he was not very big, not very tall, and dressed in white undershorts. It was not a sign of disrespect; it was the typical attire for segregated inmates—and why shouldn't it be? Their cells were stifling hot, and they rarely, if ever, saw another human being. Still, out of respect, I suppose, or maybe because it was a bit of a special occasion, Newton soon began to dress for my weekly visit: orange scrubs, the standard issue for segregated inmates on the disciplinary ranges.

Standing outside of the cell door, trying to keep my focus through the dots in the steel, made me dizzy after a while. Years later, Newton told me that it was equally dizzying looking out from the inside—why did I think it wouldn't be?

Our conversation was nearly drowned out by the *whirrrrr* of a large fan in the hallway. Outside, it was a cool autumn evening; inside, it was still stifling summer. With no natural light and an artificial light on twenty-four hours a day, segregated prisoners had no way of knowing if it was day or night. Surrounded by concrete, they didn't even know whether it was winter or summer. When I arrived from the outside world, they never asked me about the weather. It didn't matter in there.

"What does he mean by 'fortune's slaves'?" Newton asked me, looking at the paper.

I had to lean in close to hear him and I did so, fully aware of the risk and the fact that I could get in trouble if anyone were watching. (Father Bob had cautioned me to stand off to the side of the cell door, and a foot or two back.) That I got no such scolding was a good indication that no one was paying attention.

"Fortune's slaves?" I repeated, and Newton's neighbor, Green, piped up. He had also signed on for the program, and it was soon clear that he provided a healthy dose of competition for Newton.

"Fortune could be a reference to the classical idea of the Wheel of Fortune that determines man's fate regardless of his actions," he suggested. "It raises the dilemma of free choice versus predetermination."

Newton was eager to engage in a philosophical debate: "Predetermination. Is that like—"

"Oh man, that Vanna White is red hot!" another voice called out from across the range.

"I'd like to crank her wheel!"

"You got that right, bro!"

"Not *that* Wheel of Fortune, asshole!" Green shouted across the range. Then he muttered, "Freakin' psych patients."

Despite the occasional interruptions, Newton and Green's dialogue continued for some time, and I found myself reflecting that I had never heard such an enthusiastic Shakespearean discussion in any college course I'd taken or taught. In graduate school, in particular, our analysis seemed disconnected from the real world. Literary theory always struck me as too, well, theoretical. Yet here were a couple of prisoners locked away from the world, finding real-life meaning in Shakespeare's four-hundred-year-old words. I thought my Shakespeare professors would be impressed. I thought *Shakespeare* would be impressed.

"Hey! Are you guys ever going to shut the fuck up?!"

The intellectual discussion was rudely interrupted again by an angry voice from the upper range. He was offended by the intrusion of Shakespeare into the wrestling match on his TV.

"Well, not now, *no*!" Newton shouted back at the cell door, sending his voice to the upper level of the range. Then he turned to face the wall of his cell to resume his conversation with his neighbor: "So is it free will or predetermination that puts Richard in that cell, that put us in our cells...?"

Although they could not even see one another, their dialogue continued even after I gave Newton his homework assignment and said good-bye. As the range door slid open to let me out, I could still hear their voices. As I left Newton's range and headed down the hall to meet with my Shakespeare group, I couldn't help beaming as I realized that on my very first day, I had already achieved what the prisoners themselves told me was impossible: I had gotten these guys to talk about Shakespeare!

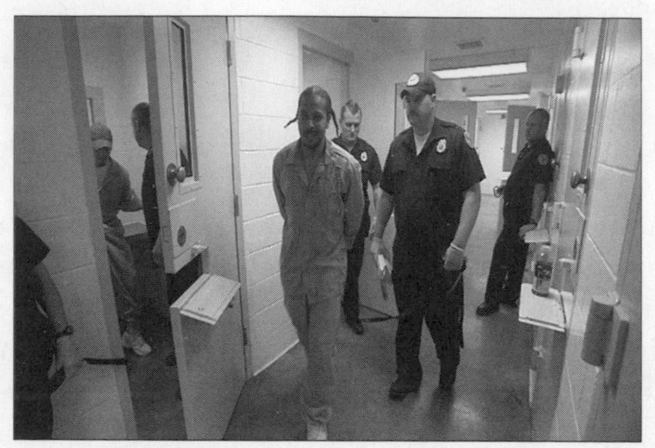

(Photo credit: Indiana State University)

CHAPTER 9

The First Group Session

Group work in solitary confinement sounds like an oxymoron, doesn't it? Selected SHU prisoners who participated in the Shakespeare program received the privilege of leaving their cells to come together for our weekly group sessions that took place in the R&R (Receiving and Release) area in the segregation unit. To get to the segregation unit from the entrance of the prison complex, I passed through a series of checkpoints, x-ray machines, metal detectors, razor-wire electrified fences, and double sets of steel doors operated under the scrutiny of armed guards in the towers. In other words, prisoners who were brought to the R&R area were still a long way from a direct escape route out of the prison. Nevertheless, because they were classified as the most dangerous prisoners in the state—and had earned that classification often through violent behavior in prison or escape attempts—any movement out of their cells was quite an ordeal.

To come to the Shakespeare group, a prisoner had to place his hands through the cuff port in his steel cell door and be handcuffed behind his back before his door was opened. He was frisked and sometimes strip-searched. With his hands and feet bound and a leather leash attached to his chains, he shuffled along, flanked by two officers, to the Shakespeare "classroom," where he was again locked into an individual cell, placing his hands through the slot to be uncuffed.

"*Shakespeare?*" said one of the officers as he walked one of my students past me on a leash. "These guys can't read Shakespeare!"

"We'll see," I answered, wondering if he'd ever read any himself.

Flurried activity crowded the narrow hallway as pairs of officers arrived one after the other, bringing all of the students to class. As each prisoner was brought into the area, I tried to step aside enough to not be in the way, but not so far as to appear intimidated. I knew that any physical contact was prohibited, so I gently declined one prisoner who extended his cuffed hands for a shake. Still, I had to reach into the prisoners' cuff ports to give them the Shakespeare pages I brought, and on my first day with the group, I wondered if any of them would try to grab my hand when I did.

When the last of the prisoners was locked into his cell, there were two prisoners on each side of the hallway, with me in the middle. As the last of the officers left the area, I was left standing there alone with no officer beside me and with four sets of eyes glaring at me. I placed a milk crate in the middle of the hallway and sat down, with my back to the open doorway. I wondered if that was a smart arrangement; down the hall to the left was the SHU kitchen, staffed by prisoners—with *knives*. But down the hall to the right was the officers' station. If, God forbid, something were to "go down," surely they would hear my cries for help. Wouldn't they?

Just then, I heard a loud *click*. The door rolled closed, and with a resounding *clang*, sealed me inside—alone—with these four prisoners.

"Okay…" I began, looking at the eyes staring at me through the opened cuff ports in the steel doors. This group included just four prisoners, but they had been selected based on a number of complicated criteria, including racial balance. There was a middle-aged black man named Thompson, a young black man named Peters, an intense white man named Hoffman, and an animated white man named Garibaldi, nicknamed Guido.

"Well," I continued hesitantly. "I'm glad you're all here."

"We're not!" said a voice from one of the slots, and the others all laughed.

"Of course, not here in the SHU, but *here* in the Shakespeare group," I restated my greeting. "So let's start with introductions. I'm Dr. Bates—"

"Ehhh, what's up, Doc?" quipped Guido, chomping an invisible carrot in a Bugs Bunny imitation. And suddenly I realized that they probably didn't know that I was a doctor of philosophy, not a medical doctor; why would they? They probably assumed that I was a psychiatrist, the type of doctor they were most accustomed to seeing there.

"I should explain," I added, "that I'm a professor—a 'doctor' of literature."

"Oh," said Guido, "so no meds, huh?"

"Right," I replied, "no meds. Just Shakespeare—that's my drug of choice."

This time, I got a laugh from the group. It felt like we were starting to warm up. The others were quieter, but Guido clearly enjoyed a chance to talk, so I started by focusing on him.

"Before I hand out your first Shakespeare assignment," I continued with a little more confidence, "I'd like to know what kind of reading you like best. I imagine you spend a lot of time reading here. Mr. Garibaldi?"

"Oh, I'm sorry, Doc," he replied in a tone that was suddenly shy. "I…can't read."

I looked at him, trying to figure out whether he was joking. I wondered if I had inadvertently invited an illiterate prisoner into the Shakespeare group. As I was pondering how to address the challenge of "reading" a Shakespeare text with someone who can't read, the others started to snicker.

"Naw, Doc," Guido confessed. "I'm joking! I can read."

Stunned to discover that long-term segregated prisoners still had a sense of humor, I found it hard to be annoyed with his constant quipping.

I handed out their first reading assignment, which they each accepted eagerly but respectfully. Through the little glass windows in the steel cell doors, I could see each man begin to look it over immediately.

For the next two hours, with no chairs in the cells, they kneeled on the concrete floor in front of the cuff ports. With the shackles still on their ankles, the prisoners communicated with one another through those little slots. Gradually, they grew accustomed to face-to-face communication, something they could not otherwise experience in the SHU. And they grew eager to begin their journey into new worlds, created some four hundred years earlier, by one William Shakespeare.

Surely, solitary confinement was the most absurd environment in which Shakespeare had ever been studied.

In the Shakespeare group sessions, I sit in between two rows of cells holding four prisoners on each side.

(Photo credits: Indiana State University)

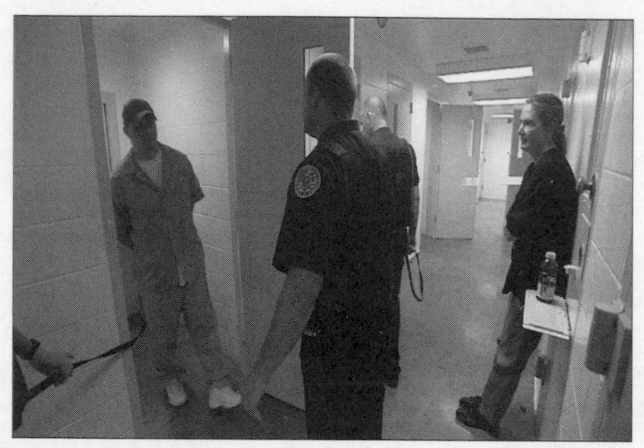

(Photo credit: Indiana State University)

CHAPTER 10

The First Lesson I Learn

"Old boy Richard was right," Newton told me when I arrived at his cell the following week.

"About what?"

"Pacing. We all do it. *Man!* Where does Shakespeare get this insight?"

I had come to prison to teach prisoners about Shakespeare, but I would learn from them at least as much as I would teach to them. "Maybe he did time in prison himself," I told him. "We just don't know much about his life at all. Some people doubt that he even existed." Then I added, "Tell me about the pacing."

"Everybody does it, even if they don't acknowledge it," Newton explained. "Just like animals. When you lock an animal in a cage, for a while it just sits there and waits, but over time, once it accepts its confinement, it starts pacing, and that's when caregivers start worrying. When tigers start to pace, it's taken the wild out of them. The psychological shift is happening. We do the same thing. If you had cameras on, you'd see that's exactly what we do: sit around a while, get involved on the range, but over time, after the novelty wears off, we start pacing—just like the cats, you know what I mean? Doing the exact same thing. Everybody paces. And that's what they're all doing: playing out these fantasies in their head. You know, like old boy Richard."

I liked the way he called King Richard "old boy." Hoping that he wouldn't see this as too personal a question, I asked him, "Would you tell me some of your fantasies?"

"Yeah, absolutely, man!" He seemed pleased to be able to talk to someone, to share his experiences. (Later I would learn that, following the hostage attempt of May 2000, he had been locked on a range all by himself and that he had spent years—literally, years—without conversing with another human being: not family, not other prisoners, and certainly not the officers. Like so many of Newton's extreme experiences, it seems impossible, but it's true.)

"I've been everything," said Newton. "I've been a bum living on the streets in New York City, I've been an outlaw in Bolivia, I've been a doctor in surgery: Dr. Newton. Yeah."

He laughed. And then he was suddenly struck by a realization.

"Hey, you know what's really cool? Here's old boy Richard in this supermax, and he's building a world inside of there with his thoughts. He's trying to make his life mean something. And then here I am—it's really cool how they mirror!—here I am, in that same little prison, trying to make my life mean something."

The parallels were striking. For years, I'd studied these plays with some of the best scholars in the world—analyzed speeches, lines, words, and even points of punctuation, from every angle of literary criticism—but I had never looked at Shakespeare through such a perspective before. I found myself wondering if anyone had.

"But mostly, these fantasies, these 'fantastical walks,' it's just really simple things, believe it or not. Hanging out with my girlfriend, seeing my mom or my brothers."

"That's it?"

"I'm telling you, man!" (My husband liked the way Newton so often addressed me, a woman, with his common expression: "man." Newton's language was an eclectic mix of street slang and self-made intellectual.) "I'm telling you, that's what everyone back here dreams of: the little white picket fence, the family, the kids. I don't care if he claims to be some great killer of the world; when you break through all that, scrape through all the bull crap, that's what he really wants. Everyone just wants to be happy."

"Have you never met anyone who found his happiness in being the great killer?"

"No, never."

He'd known more than his share of killers, so I accepted his statement as authority.

"One of the cool things I've had in my life," Newton continued, "even though I left it—it, life—so young, is that I've been out to the country, been to the ghetto, and had all these different experiences."

"So you have a rich source of fantasy material?"

"Right, yeah!" He chuckled, apparently pleased that I was beginning to think like a segregated prisoner myself. "One of the things I remember is the church environment. They'd have these big picnics, play volleyball and baseball. So I would imagine being there, but right now, not like I was ten again, but like it was right now. The kind of conversations I would have, deep kind of philosophical conversation, not the 'Oh man, I'm ready to go smoke a joint, really!'—not the kind of things that don't mean anything. Maybe it's with a student or somebody who's in college, and I would talk about Socrates and how his great claim was: 'I don't know anything.' And I would argue how knowing that in itself *is* something. Or that Nietzsche guy, I would talk about that *Twilight of the Idols* thing he wrote..."

Nietzsche? Socrates? This from a prisoner who did not even know who Shakespeare was when he first joined the program? I would later learn that prisoners' reading matter was quite eclectic. In segregation, it was largely determined by whatever was available to be circulated, illegally of course, from one prisoner to another. And Newton's neighbor was Green, the prison philosopher.

"But why does everybody *pace*?" Newton asked, more of himself than of me, and then he answered his own question. "I think it has to be attached to what goes on while pacing—exactly what Richard is doing, peopling his world, playing out fantasies, making this moment, this time, mean something. You're definitely doing as he's doing, you're peopling the world, and while pacing! Like, I can be watching a movie and I'll doze off into the fantasy I left off from yesterday, and without fail it'll pull me out of the movie I'm watching, and I'll get up and just start pacing."

"Pacing…where?" I asked, peering through the pegboard door into Newton's seven-by-nine-foot cell, thinking how bored I got walking circles on the quarter-mile track on campus.

"It's five steps, from one end of the cell to the other."

He started walking from one end of the cell to the other, counting aloud with each step: "One…two…three…four…five." He turned around, still counting: "One…two…three…four…five." He returned to face the door. "*Man!* I've counted it a million times!"

Five steps: his own "little world."

Chapter 11

Regaining Lost Humanity

Each week, I brought the prisoners another reading assignment, as well as homework questions to answer. The group session always began with each prisoner reading the homework he had written that week and all of the participants giving one another feedback. Usually, the feedback was positive, constructive, supportive. But inevitably, it also sparked discussion, and debate, about differing interpretations of key passages.

Our first text was the soliloquy of Richard the Second because I had assumed that prisoners would be able to relate to it. Instead, half of them did not believe that Richard is, literally, in prison: "This prison where I live." Instead, they insisted that Shakespeare is describing a metaphorical prison. But that is the beauty of Shakespeare: there often is more than one way of looking at the text, and I encouraged prisoners to do just that—and to respect one another's interpretations. That lesson—how to look at things from more than one perspective—was precisely what they needed.

For example, the following week, when we began to study *Macbeth*, our first full play, I raised the question, "Why did Macbeth have second thoughts about killing Duncan?" And each member of the group had a different perspective.

Guido: "Duncan's a friend, man. That's ugly."

Thompson: "We should ask, 'Why do we have second thoughts about killing someone?'"

Peters: "I'm gonna take it back to the streets. You're out there being greedy, and a guy might have more power than you, and you think, I'm gonna take this guy out, even though he's a friend—but over what? Over some poison, over reigning over some neighborhoods that don't even matter. Your name ain't ever gonna be engraved on these streets. It's just a cycle, same as Macbeth."

Hoffman: "Ultimately, here's the question Macbeth needs to face, and it's the question we all need to face: What does it profit a man if he gains the world but loses his soul? Seriously. You gain everything but you lose your humanity. This is what happens to Macbeth. And that's what happens to us, out of the choices we make."

Peters: "Straight up! Shakespeare seen this essence of life. He put in his plays how the world really is. You read his play and you're like, 'Wow, this stuff is going on! This stuff is for *real*!'"

I was impressed with the ability of the prisoners I was working with. Granted, I had some drop out from lack of interest, and other losses due to transfers. But, for the most part, I found that the prisoners who had a genuine desire to read Shakespeare were able to do so, even though many of them had limited education and little, if any, previous experience with this literature. I had assumed that we would read each scene aloud as a group and that I would have to translate the language for them. I quickly learned, however, that a university education is not a prerequisite to reading Shakespeare. After all, his original audience was not college-educated. Neither was he.

From the very first session, the prisoners let me know that reading the text out loud is a waste of their precious conversation time. From then on, the prisoners read the text individually in their cells, and each week when they came together in the group, they kept the conversation going with very little commentary from me. They raised the questions, and they answered them. I was not teaching them how to read and understand Shakespeare; they were teaching one another.

The prisoners in the group were just beginning to read, comprehend, and explore this complex text, but eventually they would create their own original adaptation not only by putting the text into their own language, but also by making the story relevant to a prison audience, placing it into a contemporary urban city setting. The following summer, another group of prisoners in open population would perform the Shakespearean adaptation written by the segregated prisoners. Videos of the performance would be broadcast on the institutional channel, so that all 2,200 prisoners in the facility could view it—including the segregated authors, who would thus be able to enjoy the fruits of their labor. This challenging, but monastic, environment offered prisoners the opportunity to closely read Shakespeare's plays and, in those extended periods of contemplative isolation, they were able to connect with the text more deeply than the average reader.

"This place is great!" Newton told me that day, gesticulating around his cell. "*Great* for reading Shakespeare!"

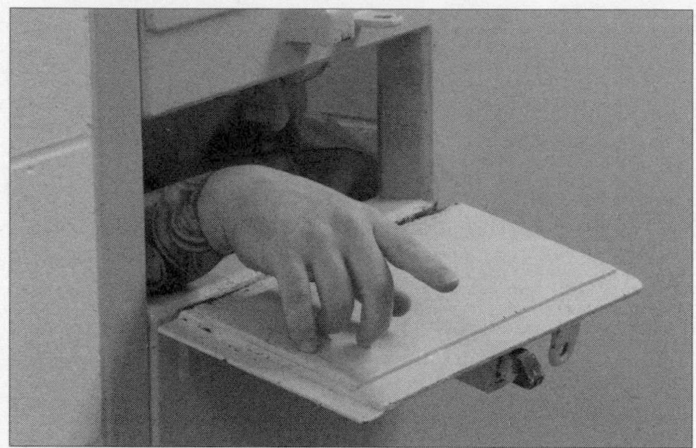

Newton through the cuff port.

(Photo credits: Jon Mac Media; Jessica Kingsley Publishers)

Chapter 12

Contraband

Each facility has a different check-in process, and in the many prisons I have either worked in or visited across the country, I have experienced everything from a full strip search to a simple computerized eyeball recognition scan. Some facilities require an officer escort or issue an emergency communication device with a panic button. Others stamp your hand with an infrared dye that is checked under a black light upon entering and exiting the facility. "My" prison had none of the above. The following was the standard check-in procedure for entering Wabash Valley Correctional Facility in the years that I worked in its SHU.

Driving into the compound required stopping at the guard's post and showing photo identification for the driver and any passengers, as well as a facility-issued parking pass for the vehicle. The car had to be fully locked and all personal possessions left there, such as purse, wallet, and, of course, cell phone. In the Visitor Processing Building, I showed my badge to the officers on duty and signed in to the certified volunteers' logbook, indicating time of arrival, purpose for the visit, and destination. Coat, shoes, book bag, and lunch sack were all placed on a table for inspection: books were leafed through, shoes were peered into, any item that looked suspicious (such as my tape recorder) was questioned and the appropriate authorization had to be confirmed each time.

Then I received a pat-down (by a same-sex officer) and walked through a metal detector while my possessions went through an x-ray machine. Once reassembled, with coat and shoes back on, I was buzzed into the first of several double-door sally ports (where the door behind you locks before the door in front of you opens) to enter the prison compound itself. Another check-in post and another set of gates brought me into the maximum-security zone of the compound, a third such set brought me into the SHU building, and a final series of gates brought me onto each range of the SHU itself. "Open locks, whoever knocks," say the witches in Shakespeare's play *Macbeth*. I have calculated that, in the decade that I spent in the SHU, I caused approximately half a million locks to be opened.

Contraband would be discovered during check-in, and I am pleased to say I was never guilty of a single transgression in that regard, whether intentional or not. But I heard of a teacher being fired for trying to bring in a birthday cake, and I chastised a new volunteer for bringing in a Halloween-size bag of candy (clearly, she was not intending to consume sixty Reese's Peanut Butter Cups herself). Pens had to be without the spring feature that could be used as a tattoo gun, and felt markers providing handy tattoo ink were also frowned upon. Beverages had to be in clear plastic containers and arrive unopened. (The reason for this rule was that one officer was found to be smuggling cell phones in his gallon-sized thermos.) Luckily, my ubiquitous vitaminwater was acceptable.

Sometimes, despite the closest scrutiny, the metal detector alarm would sound, and I had to step back out and try removing my wristwatch or belt buckle to see what was causing the alarm to register. I once brought in a new volunteer who repeatedly set off the alarm no matter what she removed. Finally, the male officer on duty said to her, "Uh, ma'am, I think I see what the problem is. Would you please cross your hands across your chest and walk through the detector sideways?"

Sure enough, the alarm was being tripped by the metal in her underwire bra.

A sign at the check-in desk at Visitor Processing clearly stated that female visitors or volunteers would not be allowed to enter the facility if they violate the Department of Corrections (DOC) dress code by wearing a short skirt, low cut blouse, spiked heels, or excessive jewelry. These restrictions seemed obvious enough, though I was surprised at times to see women arriving in these and other types of inappropriate attire.

Less obvious were some aspects of dress that I learned about only through my experiences over the years. A simple necklace or scarf can pose a strangulation risk; likewise, a tie for men. For this same reason, the DOC badge was worn with a clasp on a lapel and not on a rope around the neck. Through experience, I learned also to be aware of the distraction of bright colors in a world that is all bland.

There was the day I wore a green sweater, and a student came up to me after class and said, "Dr. Bates, I couldn't help noticing that you are wearing green, you read from a book with a green cover, and the word 'green' was mentioned in the passage you read. What does that mean?"

"It means," I replied, "that you are thinking too deeply about the coincidence."

I disregarded my own rule only once, opting to wear a bright and colorful Christmas cardigan during the holiday season that was adorned with different appliquéd characters. When I entered the classroom, I was immediately surrounded by the group of prisoners, as excited as a bunch of children on Christmas morning.

"Look," said one of them, pointing to my left sleeve. "Here's a snowman."

"Here's a Christmas tree," said one on my right.

"And here's Santa!" said a voice behind my back.

I had to take the cardigan off and return to my usual prison uniform of basic black turtleneck and jeans before I could get the group to focus on Shakespeare.

On the other hand, bland colors could get you in trouble too, if they happened to match the prison uniform of your facility. A man wearing a khaki shirt and pants would blend in with the prison population at Wabash, while a male instructor was actually stopped trying to exit another facility where the prisoner scrubs were blue jeans and a white T-shirt.

When I started teaching at the Indiana women's facility, the ladies had no prison uniforms. They dressed in street clothes, with makeup and jewelry, and I worried that they simply had to grab my badge and briefcase to walk out of the facility. The only tip-off might've been that teachers did not dress as flashy as the incarcerated women.

Finally, there was the distinctive dress of the special prisoner, whose scrubs were designed to set him apart from the general population. In the SHU, that was a jumpsuit of Day-Glo orange.

"What's the point of that?" Newton asked me. "We're not going anywhere."

"That *is* the point," I replied.

Chapter 13

Childhood

"Didn't you ever steal your mom's car or something?" Newton asked me one day, trying to see if I had any criminal activity in my background.

"We were poor," I answered, divulging some personal information despite my rule against doing so. As a teacher, I know how important it is to keep the focus on the student, and in prison even more so, but there didn't seem to be any harm in telling him, "We didn't have a car."

"Yeah, well, they wasn't so popular back in your day," Newton teased me. "What, Model T?"

True, we grew up a generation apart, but there were a number of similarities in our childhood experiences. I grew up in an inner-city ghetto, as did Newton. I was white in a black neighborhood, as was Newton. I was a scrawny insecure kid, as was Newton.

We both grew up with too little parental supervision: his mother worked day and night to avoid relying on welfare; my parents were both poor immigrants working at the same factory. My father worked the day shift, and my mother worked the night shift. They rarely saw their kids, and with only those few minutes between shifts, they rarely saw each other. Both Newton and I grew up on the streets, avoiding school much of the time—although we were both good students when we "applied" ourselves. His hangout was the underpass of the highway; mine was the public restroom in back of the Shell gas station. We both spent our share of nights quite literally on the streets. And we both ran with older crowds that served as negative role models. Criminal activity was common among his peers and mine: shoplifting, vandalism, drugs, and gang violence were part of everyday life during our elementary school years. My first boyfriend was gunned down in a drug deal gone bad. It could have been Newton who was teaching Shakespeare to me.

Growing up poor was what we had in common. Growing up loved or abused—that was the crucial difference. Newton's childhood medical records include a history of untreated serious illnesses, injuries, and malnutrition. He grew up with a teenage mother who neglected him, a stepfather who beat him, an uncle who abused him, and an older brother with a criminal record of his own.

"It was bad," Newton acknowledged, "but I think the advantage of being a kid is the lack of perspective. Unless you can compare some other great life to this bad life, you can't appreciate the distinction. If that's your life, that's your life."

He showed me a photocopy of his childhood medical record. It was compiled by his state-appointed defense lawyer at the time of his sentencing in 1995. Such an extensive history of childhood abuse would normally serve as a mitigating factor, but in Newton's case it did not.

"The one thing I remember," he said, pointing at the entries, "is all these 'missed medical appointments.' 'Follow-up not done.' 'Shots not up to date.'"

He looked at me and asked, "Is that normal?"

I shook my head.

"You know, that's why they called me Dink. I shrunk up. They thought I had cancer, but it was some kind of nickel deficiency or something. I was malnourished on my mother's milk—no joke! Anyway, I remember at my trial, the lawyer was pointing out the neglect."

At the trial, when his attorneys tried to mitigate his guilt by describing his mother's neglect, Newton sat with his fingers in his ears.

"Mom made a lot of mistakes. She never really wanted to take care of us, so she would send me to live with my aunt. She wasn't really my aunt; she was just someone willing to take care of me. And then there was this one time, I'm too young to remember, but Mom says I was being babysat and these kids strapped me down to this ironing board and they were burning my arms with the iron. She pulls up and hears me screaming from outside the house. She says both my arms were all black."

It was on the record: January 1978. He was fourteen months old.

"And then later, when I got a little older, I would run away all the time 'cause my stepdad would just beat the crap out of me. I'd be home five minutes, go to my room, and climb out the window."

"How bad were the beatings?"

"Hospitalized me twice. Welfare took me out of the house. Said they wouldn't let me back in unless he signed a paper promising not to beat me anymore. But here's the thing: he refused to sign—and they put me back in anyway!" He laughed, then turned serious again. "They got, uh, pretty bad. And once I hit the bricks, man—"

I interrupted him. "Uh, bricks...?"

"Yeah, bricks, you know, the streets. And man, once I hit the bricks, that just ended my life. It was over with! Before I was running *from* home, now I was running *to* the bricks. I had thirteen cases by the time I come to prison at the age of seventeen, and a lot of them are just plain runaways. I could go through why I kept running away, but what does that mean?

It just kind of mitigates the point. But once I did start running away, then it was the bricks. I was free! That itself was addictive. It got to the point where even when I could defend myself and fight against him, I just wanted that life. I was just free, you know what I mean? I didn't have any real responsibilities. I was an outlaw pretty much. I could do anything I wanted to. I lived with anybody I ever knew, stayed out all night, one night with this guy and another with this guy. There's some people who noticed that trend: 'I noticed that he was never at home and I wondered what was going on.' I remember one time I run away and I was walking, man. I was gonna walk all the way to Portland, Indiana. Walked all day, man, and come to a sign: Welcome to Muncie." He slapped the cuff port and laughed. "I had just walked in a big old circle around Muncie!"

Muncie, Indiana, is the small Midwestern town in which Newton was born and raised, a working-class industrial city fallen on hard economic times. It was on the streets (the "bricks") that he finally found the caring family that he never had at home.

"There's an underpass," Newton recalled, "and we slept back there: me and a bigger guy, older than me, and he's trying to cover me with his arm to keep me warm. He didn't have to do that, you know? But he did it. And, oh man! Semis waking me up all night. I still remember the sound of 'em. We'd go back behind Kmart—their deli throws out a lot of food—and we'd get our food, the best food ever 'cause it was free, not just free of price, but *free*. As crazy and dumb as that sounds, I was free."

Chapter 14
The Tragedy of Macbeth

I am afraid to think what I have done;
Look on't again I dare not.

—*Macbeth*, act 2, scene 2

I chose Shakespeare's criminal tragedy *Macbeth* as the first full play for prisoners to read because, better than any other Shakespeare play (or nearly any other work of classic literature), it gets inside the mind of a killer. Macbeth is a good man who makes a bad choice because he has, in Aristotle's terms, a "tragic flaw." My goal in presenting this play to these prisoners was not as lofty as wanting to teach them not to kill, or even to get them to do what Macbeth himself could not: "look on it [the deed] again." That idea would come later—from Newton. At the start, my goal was simple and selfish: I wanted to learn from these convicted killers whether Shakespeare's representation of murder is accurate. Whether it has verisimilitude, as they say in literary studies.

I didn't give them the full play all at once—for two reasons. One, I couldn't afford to buy twenty copies of the book. I was not only volunteering my time to this program, but I was also covering all my own expenses: reading materials, gas, a quick burger and fries munched on the road, and a bottle of vitaminwater that kept me going through the long evenings. Two, some books were contraband in supermax. I could not give a segregated prisoner a hardbound book at all; it was considered a potential weapon. (Can you imagine what *The Complete Works of Shakespeare*, at two thousand pages, might do in the wrong hands?) And I could not give him even a little paperback without going through a long series of administrative channels. It was easier, cheaper, and faster to print out one act of the play each week (along with some homework questions). This had an unforeseen added benefit: the prisoners had no way of knowing where the play was going next. It was like a TV miniseries. It was also like the experience of Shakespeare's original audience, since they didn't know how the play would end.

Newton completed the same assignments as the other prisoners by working individually in his cell and then handing in the pages to me. Very quickly, Newton's weekly inquiries grew more and more intense. For example, I gave him Shakespeare's description of the witches' brew:

Round about the cauldron go;
In the poison'd entrails throw.
Toad, that under cold stone
Days and nights has thirty-one
Swelter'd venom sleeping got,
Boil thou first i' the charmed pot.
Double, double toil and trouble;
Fire burn, and cauldron bubble.
Fillet of a fenny snake,
In the cauldron boil and bake;
Eye of newt and toe of frog,
Wool of bat and tongue of dog,
Adder's fork and blind-worm's sting,
Lizard's leg and owlet's wing,

For a charm of powerful trouble,
Like a hell-broth boil and bubble.
Double, double toil and trouble;
Fire burn, and cauldron bubble.
Scale of dragon, tooth of wolf,
Witches' mummy, maw and gulf
Of the ravin'd salt-sea shark,
Root of hemlock digg'd i' the dark,
Liver of blaspheming Jew,
Gall of goat, and slips of yew
Silver'd in the moon's eclipse,
Nose of Turk and Tartar's lips,
Finger of birth-strangled babe
Ditch-deliver'd by a drab,
Make the gruel thick and slab:
Add thereto a tiger's chaudron,
For the ingredients of our cauldron.

And he wrote:

I spent three days trying to piece together a pattern in the witches' spell, finding some hidden meaning. Would all the animal parts used in the spell equal a complete anatomy of something?

That was an original approach to this passage that I had never heard any scholar attempt. And he was scrupulous in his analysis.

First of all, the First Witch gives instruction for this charm and says, "in the poison'd entrails throw." Now, I understand "entrails" to be the "innards." And if that is the instruction, then are the ingredients mentioned all innards of that part of the anatomy? I am not guessing so, but it reads that way if it is so instructed. "Fillet" of a fenny snake; is "fillet" the head? Okay, the "blindworm" I know to be a slowworm. And my conclusion is that it is the legless lizard and not the species of skink, because the very next ingredient of the spell is the leg of a lizard. The legless lizard (slowworm) would obviously not provide a leg, so one would still be required. Why did Shakespeare not define the type of lizard that the leg was from? He obviously took care in choosing the animals. He distinguished the toad from the frog! He chose the European adder's fork and it is the only venomous British snake. Why not describe the lizard? Anyways, again with "owlet's wing." I know of two owlets: the owlet moth and the owlet frogmouth (bird). Both are winged. Which is it? My guess is that it is the owlet moth! Why? Well, the owlet frogmouth is native to the Tasmania area, so it would be an exotic ingredient, which makes sense, but the rest of the ingredients are obtainable from England. Also, because the owlet moth is a destructive moth! It devastates vegetation. That would fit the image of the ingredients.

Either he had access to a contraband encyclopedia or he had an encyclopedic mind!

Okay, scale of "dragon"; what "dragon" is referenced? Initially, one would think of a reptile, but can't it be a fish? Dragonet or dragonfish? Both are fish, and as far as I know both have scales. It makes more sense to me, as he chose these animals with some care. Now, liver of blaspheming Jew! Why the liver? Or is the greater question "blaspheming"? Liver itself makes some sense as it is disgusting and it secretes bile. Although it also detoxifies harmful substances. But as a liver, why would it matter who it comes from? So, the blaspheming Jew is the key! But why not the heart? The liver just seems out of place. Maybe that is why! It gives the ingredient greater impact on the reader. Now, nose of "Turk" and "Tartar's" lips! I cannot make it out! There are the Tartar people of Russia, who speak Turkish, so I almost make that connection to Tartar's lips. But nose of Turk is holding me from that. So, what is it?

And he concluded by pointing out an error in the great bard's words:

I have a problem with the spell! What is it, you ask? The Second Witch gives instruction for the cauldron to boil and bake! I spent an entire day seeking an accurate definition of "boil and bake"! I discussed the possibility with others gifted in the culinary arts, as well. My conclusion is that it is impossible to do both simultaneously! So, it truly is magic itself! Silly, huh? Well, that is how my mind has been overanalyzing things. I do not mind, though, as I believe it is healthy.

I think it's safe to assume that no scholar has ever analyzed that passage in such detail!

The witches present Macbeth with a prophecy that he will one day be king. They do not tell him that he needs to kill the current king, however. That idea is added by his wife, his "dearest partner in greatness." From my prisoner-students, I learned about the necessity of having a partner in crime.

We were discussing the murder of King Duncan. Macbeth leaves the scene with the two bloody daggers still in his hand. To me, that had always seemed implausible. Why would he do that? He refuses to bring them back and smear the sleeping bodyguards in order to implicate them, forcing his wife to do it. To me, that had always seemed out of character. Why would he do that? Literary analysis had never provided a good answer, but the prisoners did.

"He needs for her to get her hands dirty too," said the new student in the group named Bentley.

With a waiting list that was growing longer each week, I increased the size of the group from four to eight. It was a real effort to make their voices heard across such a large space, from one row of cells to the other, but the prisoners relished the opportunity to come together for these weekly conversations.

When Bentley made the observation about Macbeth's need for a partner in crime, the others, all serving time for murder convictions, agreed. It is easier to bear the burden of guilt, especially of such a heavy crime, my students said, with an accomplice.

"I was never a good criminal by myself," Newton once told me. "I don't think anybody is."

From stealing ice cream to committing murder, Newton never acted alone. This was true from his earliest days. Like many kids do, Newton got involved in criminal activity at the urging of his buddies.

CHAPTER 15

Supermax Kid

When did your criminal career begin?" I asked Newton when he told me that his criminal activities always involved peers.

"Oh, man," he replied, trying to recall. "I began troubles really early. I started stealing with a neighborhood kid, I would have to say around age eight. The first thing I remember stealing was money out of my mom's purse. I went to Kmart and bought Teddy Ruxpin; it had just come out. It was a bear that talked, and I thought that was the coolest thing."

"The first thing you stole was a teddy bear?"

"Yeah. Bought it with the money I stole. I can remember the first thing I stole from a store. It was one of them stores where you can buy little snacks and they had a freezer with ice cream in it. One of them had mentioned, one of my buddies, had to be one of the older ones—"

"The idea came from someone else?"

"Definitely from this guy's suggesting, 'He ain't scared, he'll do it,' or something like that. I'm bent over like this with ice cream in the waistband. I ran out the store and down the street. I didn't get away, though. He knew I stole it. I guess I got away without legal consequence, but I couldn't go back in there. I thought that sucked."

"Your motivation was to impress the older kids?"

"Definitely. 'Cause I remember him suggesting I wasn't scared and how I felt with that, even though I was scared."

"When were you first arrested?"

"Age ten. Stealing."

"What was the impact of the first arrest?"

"I mean, it made the wrong impression. I had status now. I was like, I been to Juvenile: 'Give me rank, yeah!' People looked at me different on the streets, like, 'Aw, that's Dink, man, he just got out of Juvenile!'"

Newton spent most of his childhood, from the ages of ten to seventeen, locked up in a variety of juvenile institutions.

"It does the wrong thing for a kid," he continued. "It boosts his ego on the streets. In school, too, it made 'em think you were tougher."

"Did you have the opportunity to be rehabilitated?"

"Maybe, I don't know. I mean, Juvenile is not like some school or something. It's nothing. You just sit in this big room and serve your little time, watch TV. Well, the other kids did. I didn't."

"What do you mean?"

"They always put me in isolation."

"Isolation—in a juvenile facility?"

"Yeah."

"Tell me about it," I asked. What he told me I found hard to believe—that is, until one day I actually saw it for myself.

"It's a dark cell. Man, it's the weirdest thing! It's a concrete room maybe five feet by five feet, if that, because I remember not being able to stretch out, and I was a small kid anyway. It's probably about this big." He reached out with both arms. "You could reach both walls. Solid steel door, pretty thick. There's nothing in there, just a little bitty small mat on the floor. The mattress fit exactly end to end. It's just a weird little getup, like a dog thing. It's like where you would lay a dog down. Like: 'Go to sleep!' That kind of thing."

"'Cabined, cribbed, confined'—like Macbeth says he feels. Or, maybe more like a coffin?"

"Yeah, with a real tall high ceiling. There's a light at the top, way up there. You couldn't jump and touch it, might be as high as a basketball net. And they turn it off. When you're in there it's off all the time. And there's a little space under the door, so you'd put your ear down to the door. But they'd be way far away; they wouldn't be in the dorm area. And you'd be listening, just to hear 'em, just to not feel so alone, I guess. There's probably only this much space under the door."

He held up his hand with an inch of space between his thumb and forefinger.

"As a matter of fact," he added, "there's no ventilation in there. I swear. That is absolutely true."

"Were you placed in that dark cell each time you went to Juvenile?"

"Yeah, that's where you start at, you do a little while in there when you first come in. At least, I did." He laughs. "Man, that was insane! How barbaric was that? That's where everything comes out. That's where you're tore up and going through everything. You're all by yourself, in the dark, crying. It was brutal, I think, for a kid. Man, it was brutal!"

"How long are you there?"

"I don't know. Maybe forty-eight hours."

"Were you ever let out?"

"There's a certain excitement about it: the air is different, everything is different. I don't know how often it is, but they come and get you to pee."

"Like a dog."

"Exactly. Like a dog, exactly."

"Water?"

"No, you can only get a drink when you pee."

"Were you there in summer?"

"I've been all times of year."

"Was it hot?"

"Yeah, stuffy. I remember the mattress being all sticky."

"Hot, no air, no water..."

"You're right," he said. "You wouldn't do that to a dog."

Chapter 16

The Closet

"Hey, guess what?" This time when I arrived at Newton's cell, I had some exciting news. "I'm going to Muncie! How cool is that?"

"It's real cool, man! What—what are you going to do there?" He sounded worried for a moment, then realized. "Must be going to Ball State, huh?"

"Yep, for a conference. To talk about—well, to talk about this, actually."

"The program? Wow: full circle! It's a small world, man."

I would find out just how small when a senior professor at the university approached me after my glowing report of Newton and his Shakespearean accomplishments to tell me that she recalled vividly the campus reaction to a murder of one of their students—the murder for which Newton was convicted.

What other husband but my Allan would drive across the state to enter a closet? He had been supportive of, and involved in, my prison work all along. He attended some of the group sessions, he met Newton at his cell, he listened patiently each week to my reports of what I'd learned about life in solitary confinement.

So when I said I wanted to find Newton's juvenile supermax, he was on board. This was our second trip across Indiana to Muncie in two weeks. During the conference weekend, armed with Newton's maps drawn from memory, we had located what we thought was the building—but couldn't get in. The thrift shop now occupying the former detention center (which had previously been a Catholic school) had been closed. When we arrived during the second trip, it was open.

We entered through the parking lot, as Newton said he did. We climbed up the short flight of stairs to a receiving area.

"Name!" the officer would have said to the ten-year-old Newton.

"May I help you?" the kindly gray-haired woman asked us.

"We'd just like to, uh…look around," I replied. What was I supposed to say: "I'm looking for the isolation cell where the county turned its abused children into hard-core killers"?

The detailed accuracy of Newton's pencil sketch, drawn from twenty-year-old memories, was impressive. Those events were indelibly stamped in his consciousness. Following his map, we entered the large, open auditorium that apparently served as the juveniles' day room, with a raised stage platform where the guards sat. On this day, instead of seats, the room was filled with rows upon rows of secondhand clothing: dresses, slacks, coats, hats. My husband started shopping for a leather belt, looking for a bargain.

Nervously, I ventured into the room across the hall, the former classroom that served as the dormitory for the children. It looked like just another room filled with secondhand dishes, pots, and pans. I walked up and down the aisles, but there was no sign of Newton's cell. I was beginning to feel disappointed. Maybe we had the wrong location; maybe we'd driven all this way for a thrift shop! I walked to the back of the room, turned a corner, and found it: the dark cell! Clearly, its original purpose had been as a storage closet, so there would have been no need for windows or ventilation. The thrift shop used it to store, ironically, used children's toys. I found a beat-up little teddy bear, propped him up against the brick wall, and took his picture. He looked, I don't know, scared.

I stood outside of the cell, examining its proximity to the rest of the room. There was a wall of windows that might have provided a glimmer of light in the crack under the solid steel door. But during the day, this room would've been empty. Children and officers would've been in the dayroom across the hall—too far away to hear any cries from the child locked in the storage closet.

Finally, I stepped inside, stretching out my arms to reach the walls on either side. I looked up and saw the remnants of a light fixture about as high as, yes, a basketball net. I looked down and saw the concrete pavement under the doorway scratched by what I imagined to be desperate little hands. It gave me a chill just looking at it, imagining the child who might've made those marks, imagining that it might've been Newton.

"Hey, look!"

My thoughts were interrupted by my husband entering the room, waving a brown leather belt in his hand. "Found what I was looking for."

"Yeah," I replied. "Me too."

CHAPTER 17

My Secret Life

I never told my parents about my prison work, even though I think they would have approved. Helping others was one of the values I learned from them. But I kept it as my "secret life" to avoid burdening them with worries about my safety. Those kinds of stressors had a serious impact on my mother's medical condition. After all of her wartime struggles, she was handed another burden later in life: she struggled for nearly twenty years with Parkinson's disease. In her condition, emotional equilibrium was essential, so prison was not the only thing I kept from her and my father. They did not know whenever I was ill, did not know when I had surgery, did not even know when I got married. (No one did; Allan and I eloped.)

Even if I didn't share some of these significant events in my life with them, I was close to both of my parents. I called them every day, and Allan and I traveled two hundred miles to visit them every month until they both died. I tried to support them emotionally and financially. My mother suffered a stroke just weeks after I started working at Indiana State University, and my meager part-time salary went entirely to covering her medical expenses. As my workload and salary increased, so did the medical bills, which my sister and I shared. The stressors about reaching that tenured position were directly related to my need to be able to support my parents.

As they aged, I was saddened to see how their world diminished. After experiencing several bad falls on the sidewalk, my mother stopped going for the neighborhood walks she used to enjoy. When I received my PhD, I couldn't convince her to come to my graduation in a wheelchair. My father's world revolved entirely around caring for her. When she died, he moved into a small condominium and spent the next twelve years in one lonely little room surrounded by his books in boxes that he didn't even bother to unpack. The man who had once been moved by the view from the Alps now didn't even open the curtains to look out of the window.

"Everyone just puts themselves into so many prisons," Newton had said, and it so aptly applied to my aging parents. I worried that it would apply to me as well.

As an infant, I had nearly drowned in the bathtub, and all of my life, I avoided learning how to swim. As a youth, I sat on the shore when my friends swam at the beach during high school vacations. As an adult, I sat on the shore when Allan took our grandkids tubing behind a rental boat in the summer. Would I let childhood phobias become crippling paranoias? Literally or metaphorically, how long would I continue to miss out on my day at the beach because of my fear of boats?

Chapter 18
Tough Freedoms

Before I started the program, I handed each prisoner a survey. To get to know the prisoners better, and to help determine which ones would be invited to join the program, I asked them to answer some questions about their educational background and prior experience with Shakespeare, if any.

On his survey, Newton had written:

> *The last grade that I completed was…well, I am not sure. Technically, the record should reflect that I completed the eighth grade. That is, however, a bit deceiving. I did not complete the curriculum of a class since grade five. At that point, I entered institution after institution and home after home. I do not recall spending even one month in any class since grade five. As I would leave an institution, they would just place me in a grade. So I never really graduated from grade school. I remember being in middle school and looking at the material like Homer Simpson: duh! I was out within the week.*
>
> *High school was the same way. By age fifteen, I spent the days just walking from one end of town to the other in order to pass the day and eating from large banquets of trash behind Kmart, and at night I would sleep under the overpass at the edge of town. Literally! To this day, the sound of a semitrailer takes me back to*

the interruption of sleep. I just smile, because memories of any sort are my only freedoms, and even tough "freedoms" beat captivity! That is pretty much the extent of my experience with conventional education. I came to prison at age seventeen. I never studied Shakespeare in school. He was just a one-named figure from history to me, like Moses or Hitler. I had no idea that he wrote.

After just a few months, he had grown comfortable with the language. He likened it to solving math puzzles, something he enjoyed and was very good at.

"If I say sooth, I must report they were as cannons overcharged." I read the line spoken by the soldier describing Macbeth and Banquo's actions in battle.

"'To tell the truth, it was a bit much,'" Newton translated.

He was also engaging in some pretty sophisticated analysis, picking up on details overlooked by scholars or by traditional students who cannot afford to spend days scrutinizing a short, seemingly unimportant passage like this one. And Newton's interpretation suggests that the passage contains a key to understanding Macbeth's character and the changes that his military experience have brought.

"See, they notice it," he pointed out. "The others notice it. So even though Macbeth's a killer, this is extreme behavior for him. He's a soldier, but before he was just killing the enemy; now, he's freakin' disemboweling them. Before, he might not have been able to stomach the idea of killing the king, but now he's okay with it. He sleeps fine with it."

"Nature versus nurture. That's a common argument."

"Is that still an argument?" he asks. "I mean, don't we know, really?"

"Which one is it?"

"Nurture, man!"

Like Macbeth, Newton himself was shaped by his environment.

Nurture was the dominant force, as became increasingly clear to me as he continued.

~

"I'll tell you how I lived," said Newton. "By the time I'm a teenager, I'm just a bum. All I had was two pair of jeans and one was my girlfriend's. I get drunk every day. I go round up five bucks and buy a bottle of Wild Irish Rose and a bottle of Thunderbird. And, aw man, that stuff's like liquid crack! I'm drinking that every day, every day. I'm turning into a legitimate wino, and I'm still a kid. Then I started drinking whiskey, and it's not even popular among my age group in my neighborhood. You think it's more for hillbilly guys, but I'm starting to drink whatever I can get, I don't care. I robbed a liquor store one time, I never told you? My buddy got shot. I'm in this store, and I'm stealing the liquor—not the money, the liquor."

"It didn't occur to you to take the money so you could buy more?"

"Oh, it makes perfect sense, but no, none of that. I wasn't thinking straight at that time." He pointed to a line on his juvenile record. "Like, see this charge? Strong-arm robbery. Let me tell you what happened: I'm drinking forties"—that is, forty-ounce beers—"and I'll dump the Jim Beam into that and drink it like that. I'm out here on Madison Street, where the kids cruise—they got their cars, sitting on their cars with their music—it's the strip in Muncie. We don't got no cars, we're bums, so we walk back and forth up there.

"This night, I was really blasted, really stupid drunk. I'm throwing my bottles into the street and it's a busy street, you know, I'm crazy. And I'm a celebrity up on Madison, so I'm living my status up a little bit, you know, and this lady who I knew when I was a kid, well, a younger kid, she's all excited like, 'I know him, man!' So I go over, start messing with her car, I'm looking through her CDs, and that's all I remember. Now I'm blasted so it's possible that it's different. She calls the police and says that I took 'em from her and started stomping on them. That's a Class A felony: strong-arm robbery. You take it physically, which usually entails you beating somebody, but I didn't do anything like that. But hey, I must've done something wrong 'cause as soon as I leave Madison, I see the cop cars flying down and I take off. They start chasing me, I'm running, and I hit this little bitty fence, little low fence like what you have around a shrub, and I go flying, one of my shoes goes flying, I don't know if I ever found my shoe. But there's a bunch of cops there now, so I just lay there flat, on the wet grass, I remember the wet grass on my face, and I see the lights shining. But I get away. I creep into this dude's house. Now I'm drinking with them. He's going to get into this fight, and me, I tell the idiot, 'Hell yeah, let's go, I got your back!' And as soon as we step outside, the cops swarm: 'Larry, get over here!'"

At that time in his life, when Newton was living on the streets, robbing liquor stores, getting in and out of juvenile institutions, he did get a chance to make something of his life: he received an opportunity to join the Job Corps in Wisconsin. Instead, he ended up in prison for life. Thinking about how he finally had something positive to look forward to, I asked him, "Why did you mess up again?"

"Well, because I was a really weak guy. That's the reason I felt like I had to sneak away."

"The Job Corps was going to be your attempt to escape, to sneak away, from your other life, your criminal life on the streets."

"Right, exactly. I didn't tell anyone about it. I knew it wouldn't take anything but a word from any of them people and I wouldn't have left. The problem is when we look back, we don't consider certain things. And that is that these two parts of the brain aren't really connected—the part with the 'I'm gonna get away' and the other part 'I'm in this life and gonna live this life.' They're not feuding, they're not at war, nothing. They're just two different fantasies, or ideas, so when you're in one you're not considering the other. When I'm on the street, I'm not thinking about two weeks from now. I'm only thinking right now. I think for the great deal of troubled youth, it's a common thing."

"And you told me the other day that your girlfriend was pregnant. At sixteen, were you excited about becoming a father?"

"Oh yeah, she was my girlfriend or whatever you are at that age. Yeah, that was a big deal. Yeah, man! Thing is, I knew, we knew it was between me and this other guy—he's dead now, he's the one taught me how to steal a car. I always wanted to be a father because I hated mine so much and I thought I would be a good father."

"You said 'would be.' Does that mean—"

"Right, I never got a chance. It was black, so obviously it was the other guy's."

"And what ever happened to your stepdad?"

"He died right after I got locked up that December. You know, they let me go to his funeral. There's, like, six officers, and we're in this church: there's probably freakin' two hundred black people and two white people and six cops all in the back."

"Your stepdad was black?"

"Right. And I don't know what this means psychologically, but I'm sitting there and I'm not moved by it, the funeral. It's like the whole novel experience. I'm sitting there in full trip gear—you know what that means, right? You got your hands crossed like this, chains around your wrists and your ankles, and another chain from your belly to your ankles, so you can't turn from side to side. And I've always had a problem with handcuffs. I put more pressure on them than you need to. I end up with bruises on my wrists and ankles. So I'm sitting there in full trip gear, I'm wearing prison clothes, my family around me. They're still looking at me, the officers are looking at me, and I don't know how to take it. It feels awkward, it feels weird, it feels way out of place. I'm not even thinking about him being dead."

"That's probably normal."

"Then for whatever reason, they suddenly say I have to go. They speed it up so I can go view the body. They're still talking and everything, but the officers say, 'Well, we gotta take him out of here, so he's gotta go view the body.' And I go up to the casket, it ain't no big deal, but for whatever reason just at that moment I broke down, started crying and everything. I don't know why. I think I did love the guy. I'm getting soft now thinking about it."

For a moment, he looked like he was about to break into tears, then he shook it off and continued the story.

"But the coolest thing was, as soon as I did that, everybody stood up—whoosh!—and they all lined up, giving me hugs, and I'm thinking how uncomfortable the cops were: this whole church full of black people standing up all of a sudden. Like, 'Whoa! What's going on?!' And for a second I didn't even care that I was crying, but it was only for a second. I remember everybody hugging me, my little brother hugging me, 'cause he was still small then, so he was like hugging me around my waist. It was a cool experience, man. Yeah."

He stayed quiet for a long while.

"You're reliving it?"

"Oh, I'm sorry, man. Yeah. I was just thinking. It's kinda strange, now I look at him, the circumstances of his life, that's the way he viewed the world, his people probably beat him and that taught him that's how you deal with disappointment, and in turn that taught me that's how you deal when you get angry, you lash out. It's just that earlier in my life, I hated him so much."

"I'm surprised you wanted to go to the funeral."

"I hated him, but I didn't want him to die, I don't think. But I think you go through stages with your hatreds, man. Now I look at him and I think none of the things I used to think. And nothing's changed, except the way I see the world." Silence again. "Yeah. What are we doing? Where we at? Come on, let's go somewhere before I choke up."

"The Job Corps."

"Yeah," he said. "And you know what? I still got them tickets. No joke! I pull 'em out every now and then, and just look at 'em."

"Tickets?" I asked.

And he opened up his Shakespeare folder and pulled out a couple of airplane tickets to Madison, Wisconsin. He showed them to me, then he looked at the date and quickly did the math, calculating the time between the murder and his scheduled departure date.

"Two weeks," he said. "I was two weeks away."

Chapter 19

"To Know My Deed"

Whence is that knocking?
How is't with me, when every noise appals me?
What hands are here? ha! they pluck out mine eyes.
Will all great Neptune's ocean wash this blood
Clean from my hand? No, this my hand will rather
The multitudinous seas incarnadine,
Making the green one red....
To know my deed, 'twere best not know myself.

—*Macbeth*, act 2, scene 2

When we got to the climactic scene in which Macbeth kills the king, I finally learned what Newton was in for. Of course, it was not a surprise. But it was a shock nevertheless. In his homework assignment that week, he wrote:

> *The authenticity of a murderer: WOW! That is insight! The fear and confusion, the anxiety! Even if the author has not killed, he must have been exposed to that possibility. Like attempted or was at the point of trying but could not overcome those fears and great anxiety! As Mac killed Duncan, he was just in la la land! Even forgetting to leave the weapon! Man, that is just so authentic! The detail in fears, confusion, and gut-wrenching anxiety is uncanny! I regret to say that I have experience.* ☹

There. I had the answer to my Shakespearean research question regarding verisimilitude. I could leave prison and write the articles that I needed to publish in order to apply for tenure. I could stop spending my Friday nights in solitary confinement and get back to the stack of freshman papers waiting to be graded. I could say good-bye to the prisoners, thank them for their insights, encourage them to keep reading Shakespeare on their own. Maybe donate some books. I could walk through those prison gates for the last time and be free.

But then I thought about all of these people we had locked away from the world, whom I had started to get to know: the Newtons, the Bentleys, the Greens, and even the Guidos. They had no one. They seemed to need me—or, at least, seemed to need Shakespeare. I realized that I couldn't leave—not now, maybe not ever. In a way, I started to feel like I was serving a life sentence myself.

Chapter 20

CSI: Muncie, Indiana

As I learned more about Newton's life experiences, I got even more deeply involved. I sure couldn't walk away now. In fact, I had to go further. I had to go back to Muncie one more time.

On our third visit, my husband and I spent the entire day researching Newton in the archives of the *Muncie Star* and in courtroom transcripts. On September 26, 1994, the headlines read:

BSU student murdered

Man shot to death near campus

Community shocked

Victim identified, but many questions remain

Two days later, more headlines:

3 held in "senseless" killing

Suspects have long history of troubles with the law

Life of misery ended in another's death

Going through these records, I started to feel like a crime scene investigator. As a professor of literature, I was accustomed to wading through stacks of papers filled with academic jargon, but these documents took me to a whole new world. I felt uncomfortable and more than a little fearful of what I might find. The descriptions of the murder scene were especially unnerving.

Newton had entered a guilty plea at his mother's urging because he was being threatened with the death penalty. But I wasn't convinced that he was the one who actually committed the murder. The newspaper accounts, as well as what I'd learned of Newton himself, suggested that, on this day, at this particular desperate time in his life (his stepfather was dying, his mother had kicked him out, and his girlfriend left him, taking the baby that Newton had hoped was his), he would have been too incapacitated by drugs and alcohol to stand, much less accurately aim a gun he'd never used before.

Not that it matters in legal terms: in the state of Indiana, the accomplice in a murder conviction receives the same sentence, so Newton's partner was serving life as well. I just wanted to know. I needed to know. I left the office of the *Muncie Star* with two briefcases jammed full of photocopied articles to pore over.

Next, we drove through all of the worst neighborhoods in Muncie, piecing together the jigsaw puzzle of Newton's childhood: his homes, his schools, his juvenile detention centers. The stores he shoplifted from, the highway underpass where he slept, the Dumpsters he ate out of. The part of town where he grew up, known as Whitely, is a poor, predominantly black area, where liquor stores and abandoned buildings are common sights. Both my husband and I have lived in areas like this, so we felt comfortable walking those neighborhoods.

"Before we head back home," I told my husband, "there's one last place I need to see." Of course, he knew what it was: a particular alley where I could retrace Newton's—and the victim's—last steps. The articles described the victim, Christopher J. Coyle, as a nineteen-year-old white male, a good-intentioned college student who was walking a female home after a party at 3 a.m.

"You sure you want to go there?" he asked.

"Sure," I replied, exaggerating greatly. I didn't feel comfortable about it at all.

"It's just an alley," he said.

"No," I replied, "it's…it's…"

"It's what?"

"I don't know," I said. "But it's important."

We drove across town to the "good" side of Muncie. The houses were bigger; the front yards were filled with flowers instead of trash. There were attractive parks along the river; a poster announced an upcoming arts festival. Paraphrasing Dorothy in *The Wizard of Oz*, I said to my husband, "I don't think we're in Whitely anymore."

The campus influence permeated the neighborhood: frat houses, dormitories, and the large sprawling campus itself. It was not hard to imagine how all of this must've looked to the dropouts from the ghetto—and how they must have appeared to the college population.

I tried to piece out our journey using references from a number of articles—there were hundreds of articles—and a map of Muncie that we picked up at the visitor information center. Somehow, I didn't think this was the kind of tourist site they had in mind.

"Turn left—no, right," I said, testing the patience of even my supportive husband, my "partner in crime."

"We've been down this road before," he said. "We're just going around in circles."

"Uh, let me see," I replied while checking the map.

"You know, if you can't find it…" he started to state the

obvious: we should just give up and head home. But before he could finish his sentence…

"Stop!" I shouted. "There!"

The alley: uncanny, unmistakable—unfortunately.

"Oh…my…god."

In my mind, I was envisioning the murder scene: the young man stepping out of the car, the others coming up behind him, the gunshots. I'd spent so many years working with convicted criminals, but this was the closest I'd ever come to a victim. I wasn't ready for that; it was deeply disturbing.

We were still stopped at the entry to the alley. I was still lost in thought.

"You all right?" my husband finally asked.

"That's what the articles said that Newton's partner said to him," I replied. "Ten years ago. Right here."

"Said what?" he asked.

"'You all right?'"

The alley.

Chapter 21

Death Penalty

September 1995. One year had passed since his arrest. Newton sat in the Delaware County jail as the trial continued. Now the headlines read:

Teen could face death

Newton fails to stop death penalty bid

Killer's fate weighed by judge

Superior Court Judge Robert Barnet Jr. was up for reelection, and his platform was "get tough on crime." "I don't care if he is a juvenile!" seemed to be his feeling. According to newspaper accounts, when the prosecution filed the death penalty, the judge turned to the teenager with these words: "Frankly, Mr. Newton, I don't believe you have a conscience." Pressured by his mother, Newton agreed to plea-bargain into a sentence of life without the possibility of parole; furthermore, he agreed to waive his right ever to appeal the sentence in a court of law. At the age of seventeen, he wasn't even old enough to buy a pack of cigarettes, but he could legally sign away his life.

"What did you think when the death penalty was filed against you?" I asked Newton. I expected a big, dramatic revelation, but he surprised me with an understated reply.

"I really don't know," he said. "I say that I didn't care, but I must have cared."

I was dumbfounded. How could a seventeen-year-old kid have no reaction to being told that he was going to be executed? What could that tell us about the condition of his mental faculties at that time?

"And you know what?" he continued. "It made such an impression in the jail! That's like street cred. I might have been basking in it a little bit. Like, 'Yeah, man, death penalty!'"

"But when you're alone, lying awake at night...?"

"I think you just avoid it. I don't remember ever sitting down and facing it."

"Was it a surprise?"

"I knew it was coming, but it was a surprise to know that it was coming; does that make sense? When they announced it, I already knew they were going to announce it. It was brought up from the time I was arrested. They threatened my mom with that: 'They're gonna kill him!' Which is illegal."

"So it was part of your consciousness all along, but do you think you held on to some kind of subconscious hope?"

"Oh, I can say that! I can say that even years later in prison, it never sunk in. I think that little kid in me must've thought that things were just gonna work out okay. It wasn't till years later, I was in seg already, a few years into seg, maybe five years into my bit, that I realized, man, things aren't going to work out. I remember that moment, the feeling of it, like, 'Man, this is a life sentence. It's not gonna heal itself.' Because I must've felt through the whole process that things will work out, things just do." He laughed. "But, yeah, you're right. I must've had that hope somehow."

"How long did you live with the death penalty?"

"Probably a year. Yeah, it was a long time. When you get a capital sentence, you automatically go through the review process. You're pretty much on hold until it's through the court of appeals, Supreme Court. So they sent me as safekeeping to prison already. I remember when I was there, I had this crazy nightmare. I had read a Dean Koontz book called *Mr. Murder.*"

"You're in prison for murder, and you're reading a book called *Mr. Murder*?"

"Right. This guy is like some weird android-type thing. He's just this killer, man, he's hired to kill people. Then he wanders off and tries to take over the life of this other guy. I'm having this dream that he's chasing me, trying to kill me, and I'm trying to get away from him. And I wake up, I really wake up, in my cell, but my body won't move! My body was paralyzed; my mind was awake. And this will make you think it was a dream within a dream: he was still talking to me, he was still threatening me. And I still couldn't move, that's why it was so scary 'cause he's back here, which was probably just in my head—well, obviously, it was just in my head—but he's back here, so you can't see or defend yourself. It was one of the coolest dreams I ever had. I like nightmares. I like ones that you're the most active in. I like waking up and having to look around the cell, even though I know there's nothing there. I love those dreams, man!"

"Eventually the death sentence was commuted to life without parole—still an unusually severe sentence for a juvenile. Why did you give up your right to even try to appeal?" I asked.

"Hey, I was a stupid little kid, a moron, just a dumb, little punk kid. I don't even think any of this is real. I still thought I was going home. Deep down inside. It's like Boys' School: ah,

I'll be out in six months! I never took it seriously, not until I was in prison. I was already in seg when it hit me: 'Man, I got *life* in prison!' All along I thought somebody was gonna fix it. It's dumb and it's my own fault. Obviously, they meant life in prison. But it never sunk in. Besides, I thought I knew how I'd end up."

"How?" I asked.

"Executed," he replied. "Or gunned down in an escape attempt."

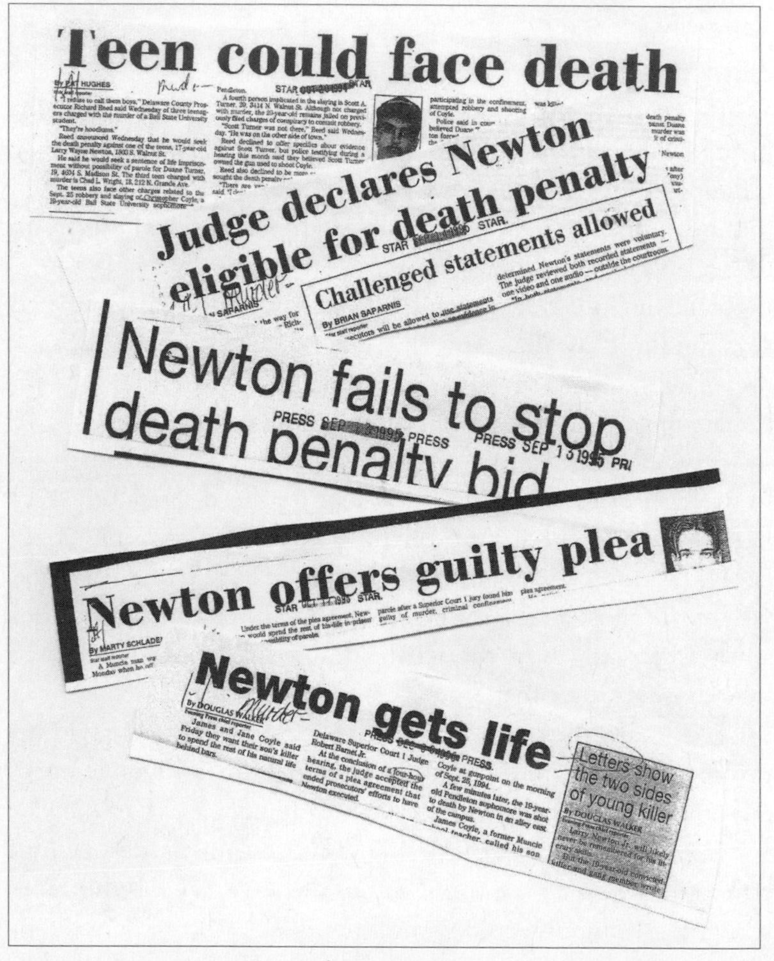

Teen could face death

By PAT HUGHES

"I refuse to call them boys," Delaware County Prosecutor Richard Reed said Wednesday of three teenagers charged with the murder of a Ball State University student.

"They're hoodlums."

Reed announced Wednesday that he would seek the death penalty against one of the teens, 17-year-old Larry Wayne Newton, 1800 S. Walnut St.

He said he would seek a sentence of life imprisonment without possibility of parole for Duane Turner, 19, 4604 S. Madison St. The third teen charged with murder is Chad L. Wright, 18, 212 N. Grande Ave.

The teens also face other charges related to the Sept. 25 robbery and slaying of Christopher Coyle, a 19-year-old Ball State University sophomore

Pendleton.

A fourth person implicated in the slaying is Scott A. Turner, 20, 3414 N. Walnut St. Although not charged with murder, the 20-year-old remains jailed on previously filed charges of conspiracy to commit robbery.

"Scott Turner was not there," Reed said Wednesday. "He was on the other side of town."

Reed declined to offer specifics about evidence against Scott Turner, but police testifying during a hearing this month said they believed Scott Turner owned the gun used to shoot Coyle.

Reed also declined to be more ...

participating in the confinement, attempted robbery and shooting of Coyle.

Judge declares Newton eligible for death penalty

Challenged statements allowed

By BRIAN SAPARNIS

determined Newton's statements were voluntary. The judge reviewed both recorded statements — one video and one audio — outside the courtroom.

Newton fails to stop death penalty bid

Newton offers guilty plea

By MARTY SCHLADEN

Newton gets life

By DOUGLAS WALKER

James and Jane Coyle said Friday they want their son's killer to spend the rest of his natural life behind bars.

Delaware Superior Court 1 Judge Robert Barnet Jr.

At the conclusion of a four-hour hearing, the judge accepted the terms of a plea agreement that ended prosecutors' efforts to have Newton executed.

Coyle at gunpoint on the morning of Sept. 25, 1994.

A few minutes later, the 19-year-old Pendleton sophomore was shot to death by Newton in an alley east of the campus.

James Coyle, a former Muncie ... school teacher, called his son

Letters show the two sides of young killer

By DOUGLAS WALKER

Larry Newton Jr. will likely never be remembered for his literary skills.

But the 19-year-old convicted killer and gang member wrote

Chapter 22

Escape Artist

The idea of being gunned down in an escape attempt was not just some dramatic fantasy. Newton had an extensive history of escape attempts that began when he was still a juvenile.

"I escaped from all them places," he said. "Every one of them: Children's Home. Youth Service Bureau. Juvenile Detention Center. Indiana Boys' School. Two from each. Total of eight."

"Your first escape, from Children's Home, how old were you?"

"Probably thirteen. I was with a couple of older kids. The first time, I left from school, me and another guy. Just walked off. The second time, we cut the alarm on the exit door."

"So then they sent you to the Youth Service Bureau."

"That was a step up from Children's Home, more isolated, more intense. First time, we just walked off from school. The other time, me and two other guys—they were older than me, they're closing in on eighteen and I'm just barely fourteen—we cut the alarm wires on the exit door in the back of the building. It was January. We were just freakin' walking out on the highway. I'm cold, I'm wet, don't know even where we're at."

"Next you're sent to Juvenile Detention Center."

"That's where you wait on your court, it's like being in jail without bond. When you go outside, you're shackled, handcuffed, it's the prison for kids. Harder to escape—but I did. The first time, we took out the screws on the window. The second, we climbed the fence. It was intense, man! Here's how it happened: We was out playing ball and we go to the guards like, 'How about a game?' And we kinda weed out, let the other guys play with them, get 'em distracted, and then we just took off, got up the fence, a good twenty-foot fence, barbed wire, and just outrun them. They chased us down, and I remember I was running in these bright orange shoes. And this crazy woman yelling through the neighborhood: 'Aw, Dink just escaped out of Juvenile!' So I jumped in a Dumpster and I hid in there for a couple of hours."

"Then you're sent to Indiana Boys' School. That's a much bigger deal."

"Let me tell you how it works: if you're crazy bad, you get six months; otherwise, it's ninety days. I did over a year! I went twice—that's what they call the young supermax, the lockdown unit. In fact, it may be even more locked down than adult supermax: you don't have TV, radio, none of that stuff. You're in a cell twenty-three hours a day, by yourself. I spent probably four months of that year on R.U."

"How did you escape from Boys' School?"

"The first time, really, I had done good, and I got to go home on the weekend. Once I got around my buddies, I never went back. So that was my first escape. The second, I just walked off campus. Me and this other guy. That's the weirdest thing. Good thieves can go into buildings and act like they belong there, you know what I mean? They can walk in every restricted area. If they got the demeanor that they belong there, nobody questions them. I walked off campus like that. And you're way out in the country. I was hiding in a shed. All these country bumpkins, you think—boom!—they're gonna kill you."

"You've got two adult escapes, both from supermax."

"The first one isn't really an escape. But I was digging holes, so yeah, I guess that is 'escape'; what else would it be? And it's not like I wasn't testing the material. I cut into the chase way."

(The chase way was a small opening that connected the venting system throughout the prison. Newton had actually starved himself to become small enough to fit into this opening.)

"For whatever reason," he continued, "they had the unlocked part on the inside, and once you get to that stage, there was a door and you were out! You had to get the bar off the back board; it's a little tricky but I had it figured out."

He looked at me and laughed. "Is it hard for you to get into the mind-set?"

I shook my head. I didn't think it was hard to imagine a lifer wanting to get out of prison, by whatever means. "Did you actually get out?" I asked.

"Technically. Just into the chase way. I'll tell you how I got busted—it's the coolest thing ever. I take the vent off and I take a piece of paper and draw little black circles on it so it looks just like the vent. You really have to get close to see it's just a drawing. And all the mortar I took out, I took toilet paper and toothpaste to fill in. One day there's a shakedown, everything's cool, we pass. I'm getting cuffed up and everything to go back to the cell, and there's a guy complaining: 'Hey, ain't supposed to take the radio!' Brings the sarge in, and sarge figures he may as well look around, so just as they roll my door, sarge, he just kind of peeks into my cell, gets up on the toilet, as he goes to brace himself, his hand pushes in on the paper, and he goes, 'Whoa! Whoa!' and he sees it goes right through to my neighbor's cell. It was pretty funny. So that was the first attempt."

"How did you get to do it again?"

"Well, it's 'cause they're really smart people."

"Same cell?"

"No, but upstairs, directly above my buddy's cell. This is a funny story too. I get some saw blades from a buddy, cut the entire light off, but I'm short, I'm trying to jump off the bed and take a cut each time."

"No cameras?"

"No cameras. I get all the guts out, took nine days, but the back panel of the light I can't reach, so I figure I'll kick my leg up in there and kick the back end in, and I'm stronger than I think. I kick it and the whole panel just flies off onto the chase way, hitting every pipe and wall in the thing, big metal aluminum thing: *ding ding ding ding*! The whole range went dead silent. I stood there for like two hours not knowing what to do. Eventually, I get enough courage to climb in there to get it, so then we're ready but we can't leave till night. My buddy tells his buddy that we're ready to go, and this guy, he sees an opportunity to get brownie points so he puts a little slip in his mail bag."

A prison snitch.

"Pretty soon," Newton said, "I hear somebody downstairs say, 'Hey man, look out the window at all these dudes with guns,' and I know it's one of them squads. I know we're busted. Yeah."

He laughed.

"That would've got you all the way out, to the street?"

"Yeah. I woulda made it," he said with certainty. Then he opened up his Shakespeare homework.

"Good thing I didn't."

Chapter 23

The Dagger I See before Me

Is this a dagger which I see before me,
The handle toward my hand? Come, let me clutch thee.
I have thee not, and yet I see thee still.
Art thou not, fatal vision, sensible
To feeling as to sight? or art thou but
A dagger of the mind, a false creation,
Proceeding from the heat-oppressed brain?
I see thee yet, in form as palpable
As this which now I draw.
Thou marshall'st me the way that I was going;
And such an instrument I was to use.
Mine eyes are made the fools o' the other senses,
Or else worth all the rest; I see thee still,
And on thy blade and dudgeon gouts of blood,
Which was not so before. There's no such thing:
It is the bloody business which informs
Thus to mine eyes. Now o'er the one halfworld
Nature seems dead, and wicked dreams abuse
The curtain'd sleep; witchcraft celebrates
Pale Hecate's offerings, and wither'd murder,
Alarum'd by his sentinel, the wolf,
Who howls his watch, thus with his stealthy pace.

With Tarquin's ravishing strides, towards his design
Moves like a ghost. Thou sure and firm-set earth,
Hear not my steps, which way they walk, for fear
Thy very stones prate of my whereabout,
And take the present horror from the time,
Which now suits with it. Whiles I threat, he lives:
[A bell rings.]
Words to the heat of deeds too cold breath gives.
I go, and it is done; the bell invites me.
Hear it not, Duncan; for it is a knell
That summons thee to heaven or to hell.

—*Macbeth,* act 2, scene 1

Lee Bentley, the latest addition to our group, joined not out of any interest in Shakespeare but because of his interest in rap music. He knew that his hero, Tupac Shakur, had studied the bard's work. A poet himself, Bentley enjoyed adapting key speeches from *Macbeth* using contemporary hip-hop language. And he was good. In his rendition of the hallucination that leads Macbeth to murder King Duncan, the dagger becomes a pistol, but much of Shakespeare's original language is echoed in the contemporary translation. In addition, he retains the seductive quality of the weapon that attracts the killer to it:

What is this?
Are you the vision I've seen in my thoughts,
reflecting the face of death from your chrome skin?
Come on, baby, let me hold you, yeahhh!—but my palm feels nothing!
My mind is playing tricks on me, due to the drama I know I must face tonite.
I see this pistol again, as vivid as a movie scene,
like the one against my waistband now, that I draw upon the shadows.

It is leading me deeper into darkness,
to stumble into bloody puddles that are deeper than the ocean.
I still see it!
And now, on her chrome face and firm backside are splashes of blood,
and her mouth moans with the satisfaction of our secret affair.
This can't be real!
It must be the bloody wickedness that I am about to commit
to someone who thinks I'm his friend.
This visual poetry is already writing a part of me dead:
the voodoo of those strange sistas.
And now I must hold her hips to the music of murder,
but slowly, slowly, like the spider whose web already shakes with its victim,
not to rattle the fly tangled in the web.
I must go, to take destiny's hand: the bell invites my trigger finger to coil like a snake.
If Duncan only knew that bell is summoning his soul
to the kiss of the longing lips of death.

In the group sessions, I listened to Bentley read his poetry, and then at his cell, I listened to Newton read his analysis. I couldn't wait until I would be able to bring the two of them together.

(Photo credit: Indiana State University)

Chapter 24

The Shower: Newton

Before killing the king, Macbeth's conscience conjures up the frightening image of a bloody dagger. He should be repelled by it, but he reaches toward it. Trying to understand the killer's motivation, I asked Newton, "Is that evidence that he is not looking for a way out of doing the deed, but a way in?"

"A way in, absolutely!" he agreed. Then he added, "'Cause, hey, you know what? I had a 'bloody dagger,' but not a bloody dagger. I'm not doing anything like, 'Is this a gun I see?' But I am acting out the deed psychologically: I jump out of the car and just start shooting. I'm trying to build myself up, trying to pull myself into the deed, 'cause the pull is way stronger to get the hell out of there. So that's my 'dagger,' that's what I have to do to get me in there to do it. So I am kind of seeing my own dagger. It's the scene, and it's bloody."

"Like Macbeth's dagger, it's bloody?"

"Yes! Absolutely, man! But it's *different*! It's different! I mean, look, it's a *gun*! A stabbing killing, there's much more gore and blood. Shooting somebody is not nearly…I can tell you, it's probably easier to shoot somebody than it is to stab somebody, like I did in the shower at Michigan City. That was a lot harder."

"In that incident, did you see a dagger?"

"Yes! I did, man! No joke! All the way up! It started to fade out only when I actually went into the shower. Until that point, I'm walking back and forth on the range, and in my mind, I'm going through it over and over, till I go to do it, and that's when I lose the visualization."

"Does the vision convince you—and Macbeth—to do the deed?"

"Right, yeah. It builds your confidence. Or it may just keep your brain so occupied so that it don't let the doubts creep in, 'cause it don't take a lot for that doubt to pull you all the way out. It don't necessarily attract you to the deed, but maybe it makes you committed to it. It blocks everything out so all you think about is the deed: the deed, the deed, the deed."

"Macbeth sees the dagger, but he doesn't see Duncan. Did you visualize your victim?"

"No, it's just the deed. It's the attack, my part of this. I'm not even visualizing how he'd try to get away as strategies to stop him. It don't even cross my mind that he's gonna fight for his life. I'm not seeing him being stabbed; I'm seeing me stabbing."

"If Macbeth wanted to kill Duncan in the most efficient, most merciful manner—"

"He would stab him once, through the heart."

"But he uses two daggers."

"That's a butchering! But you know what, I'm just thinking: I went into that stabbing with two knives. Why did I think I needed two knives? I don't know, man, I don't know. I had never done anything like that," he said, and then added, "Or maybe I *am* Macbeth!"

"Could Macbeth be so disoriented that he'd leave the scene with the daggers still in his hand, and not even be aware that he has them?"

"Yes! I can absolutely see Macbeth having the daggers and not being aware of it! I never thought about this before—and I never told you, because I never linked these two things, but that's the cool thing about reliving it—but I remember the stabbing that I did in the shower at Michigan City. When I left the shower, I still had the knife in my hand! I swear, man! No joke! I still had the knife! Just like Macbeth—wow! It wasn't until another guy, in his cell, pointed it out to me that I was even aware of it. By then, I was all the way down the range! And then I tried to drop it and kick it towards the cells. I remember—*boom!*—dropping it. And that's when I noticed I was being sprayed. There were like thirty officers on the walks spraying me with their mace while I was stabbing the guy, but it didn't affect me then. I didn't even notice it until I was on the range and the guy told me that I still had the knife in my hand."

"What did you have against this guy?"

"What do you mean?"

"Why were you trying to kill him?"

"I wasn't trying to kill him."

This was one of my many prison moments when I'm sure I must have had a look of confused naïveté on my face as I stammered, "But, but you—"

"Look," Newton explained. "It's really hard to kill someone by stabbing. Most stabbings don't result in death. It's not like Macbeth."

And that made me recall Newton's earlier observation that he didn't believe that the kingship was Macbeth's motivation in killing King Duncan, that it was really something else that he was after. So I asked Newton, "What were you after?"

"Seg at Michigan City is a dangerous place," he replied. "Really dangerous. And remember, this is my first adult prison experience. I was still young, nineteen years old, 155 pounds, a skinny white kid. They were all bigger than me. I was just trying to make an impression. The guy, my victim, he had got this other guy, caught him blinded and hurt him real bad, so he knew that people were after him. I go into the shower, fully dressed. I got my hand in my pocket, and I see he's standing with his back to the wall. I come up and hit him in the right shoulder with the weapon in my right hand, and it's a big fat weapon, it's not a blade. I didn't know what I was doing. I'd never done anything like that before. I assumed the bigger, the better, but actually if you want to hurt somebody, it's the smaller, the better; it's hard to get it in somebody and keep pulling it out."

He looked at me to be sure that I was okay with the details before he continued.

"Eventually, it got stuck between his ribs, I couldn't get it out, so I pulled my hand back to my pocket to get my other one, and stabbed myself. And that's what took me out of that single-minded, focused, B-lined kind of behavior, and I started noticing other things. I noticed the whole area was full of COs [corrections officers] yelling, 'Stop!' And when I come out of the shower, I remember my clothes were covered with blood, but most of it was from my own cut. I lost so much blood that when I went for x-rays, I passed out in the chair."

"It would've been funny if you died," I said, wondering if he would laugh or take offense.

He laughed. "Wouldn't it?" he said. "Yeah, man, I agree: 'Died of a self-inflicted knife wound stabbing someone else.'"

He stopped laughing. "You reap what you sow."

Chapter 25

The Shower: Me

I had a shower incident of my own when I had been working in supermax for just half a year. I was feeling more familiar with the SHU—perhaps too familiar. Sometimes I would catch a range door left open if chow or mail had recently been delivered, and walk onto the range without even letting the officer in the pod know that I was there. That backfired on me more than once. The first time, I got locked in. The second time, I could've been killed.

I was talking to a prisoner in cell 11, the penultimate cell, on the second level of the range. This was the most dangerous location on any range, as it required walking past every cell, upstairs and downstairs, on your way in and again on your way out. On this particular day, I found the range door open, so I slipped in unannounced and made my way upstairs. I was unaware that there happened to be a prisoner in the upstairs shower, which was located just past cell 12. Normally, prisoners were cuffed and chained and escorted by two officers even for the short walk from their cell to the shower. But, as I was talking to the prisoner in cell 11, I heard the shower door roll open—with no officer on the range. Suddenly, I realized what that meant: I was about to come face-to-face with a naked killer.

Think quick: what would *you* do? Let me emphasize that I

do not assume that every prisoner in supermax is a crazed killer eager for any opportunity to kill again. However, in those days, most of the prisoners in long-term segregation (70 percent to be exact) were "crazed"—literally, psych patients. And even if this man did not want to kill or rape, how could he "save face" among his peers if—faced with the opportunity to assault a female on the range—he simply said, "Excuse me, ma'am," and walked on by?

Newton had recently told me that few prisoners are motivated just by a desire to hurt people, that most "troubles" happen because of peer pressure, the need to look tough in front of others, something that is especially important in a tough prison environment. When that shower door rolled open, I bet my life that he was right. The prisoner in the shower was from cell 12; I knew that because his cell door was open. In that, I was lucky: he wouldn't have to walk past me to get to his cell. If I could avoid any response to his presence, he would have the opportunity to slip into his cell without his peers knowing that he had given up the opportunity for an assault. Hard as it was, I kept my focus intently on cell 11, keeping up our conversation about Macbeth: "Why do you think Macbeth did not stop killing after the murder of King Duncan?" I asked cell 11.

From the corner of my eye, I could see the man step out of the shower. Upon catching sight of me, he did a double take. Clearly, he was facing a "first" in his life as well. He stood there, as if frozen, and finally—after what seemed like a year later!—he turned and walked into his cell. As his door rolled closed with a loud *clang*, cell 11 gave me a startled look, suddenly aware of what had happened. I finished our conversation with a quote from Macbeth: "Tomorrow and tomorrow and tomorrow creeps in its petty pace to the last syllable of recorded time."

And I left the range with a sigh of relief.

Chapter 26

All Hands on Deck

Working in supermax presented its own unique learning curve. For example, here's something that a teacher in a normal classroom doesn't usually encounter: masturbation. Seated in an open classroom, fully visible not only to the teacher, but also to his classmates, a student is unlikely to drop his drawers and expose himself. But the setting of my SHU classroom revealed only the student's eyes and a partial view of his face. I could see the prisoner's hands only when he reached out through the opened cuff port to catch my attention in an approximation of a student raising his hand in a traditional classroom. Or if he held a paper in his hands as he read from it or gesticulated toward another student in enthusiasm for (or rejection of) a comment that was made. But in all of those instances, I rarely, if ever, saw both of the prisoner's hands. They could be doing...anything.

This was, in fact, what I learned one day as I was walking from one cuff port to the next, collecting papers at the end of our session. It had been a very focused discussion, in which each of the students had been actively engaged. So it came as a bit of a shock to me to peer into one of the cells through that little window in the door and realize that one student had other—shall we say, non-Shakespearean—thoughts in mind.

As with the shower incident of the previous chapter, this was a moment requiring a quick—and appropriate—response. Again I opted not to go public with this man's very private behavior. But when the officers arrived to bring the prisoners back to their cells, I retained this particular student till the last so that we had a chance for a private conversation.

"This is unacceptable," I said to him.

"I don't mean no disrespect," he said, and I believed him. "It's just been so long since I've even seen a woman." And then he surprised me again by adding, "Besides, they're all doing it."

I had to acknowledge that that was possible, but, I hoped, not true. At least I could hope that it wasn't *all* of them.

"I'm not going to tell the others why, but next week, you will not be allowed to come to the class. If, the following week, you are able to keep your mind—and your hands—on your Shakespeare work, then I will give you another chance. But if you return and do this again, then I will inform the officers and publicly remove you in the middle of the class. Do you understand?"

"Yes, ma'am," he replied.

Two weeks later, he returned to class, and I was never aware of any further misbehavior.

This is one aspect of working in a men's prison that causes female staff, as well as volunteers, a lot of concern. I thought I had handled it very smoothly, addressing the problem without anyone even being aware of the situation. At least, that's what I thought...until three years later when Newton said to me: "Hey, did old boy Guido ever, you know, do anything back there in the SHU?"

"Uh, what do you mean?" I asked.

"Well, I don't know," he replied. "It's just that I remember this one time, when I was still back there in the group, when you looked into his cell, you had this strange look on your face, and I just imagined that he was lying there in the cell, buck naked."

Chapter 27
The Boat

One day, Newton said to me, "Can I ask you something?" and I knew it was not going to be about Shakespeare.

"No personal questions," I repeated my familiar refrain.

"I'm not going 'personal' or anything."

I looked at him skeptically.

"Do you guys have a boat?" he asked.

I was right; this was not going to be about Shakespeare.

"You should get a boat," he said, smiling as if he had just solved some great problem in my life. And, although I didn't know it at the time, he had.

"A boat," I repeated.

"Or maybe a porch swing."

It might seem an incongruous statement, but I could see the similarity. Still, I asked, "Is that as good as a boat?"

"Yeah," he nodded, smiling, lost in a fantasy image. "That's almost as good as a boat."

"Well, get off the boat and back into the book," I said, shoving his paperback copy of *The Complete Works of Shakespeare* toward him on his opened cuff port. (SHU prisoners were allowed to purchase books for themselves if they were sent directly from the publisher, and it was no small gesture that Newton spent the equivalent of his life's savings on that book.)

He was still smiling, thinking about something non-Shakespearean at that moment.

"The boat is my liberty," he said.

"*Shakespeare* is your liberty," I replied.

"That's true. Shakespeare is my liberty."

He was speaking metaphorically about "the boat," of course, but he made me start to think about boating literally. Because of our "no personal questions" rule, he couldn't know about my lifelong fear of boats, and even of water.

"Come on, man," I could hear him saying, "that's retarded!"

A boat was not my ideal of liberty. Or…was it?

To Newton, it was a metaphor, and maybe it was for me too. Of course I could spend my entire life never stepping onto a boat; plenty of people do. But I started to realize that, for me, "boat" was a metaphor for other unfounded fears. And as I aged, I worried that these fears would increasingly shut down and narrow my life—as their own fears had done for both of my parents. I didn't necessarily want to go skydiving at the age of ninety, but I did want my life to expand with each passing year, rather than narrow. I wanted to avoid spending my life in a prison of my own making.

"People just put themselves into so many prisons," Newton liked to say.

Was fear of boats one of my prisons? Would overcoming that fear set me free?

Chapter 28

New Directions

When I started the Shakespeare program, I had intended to do it for just one year, but we were on an unstoppable roll: our successes had impressed the prison administration and had even been noted by the local media. My prison work added another dimension to my personal life as well. The prisoners introduced me to rap music, informing me that Tupac Shakur had been a fan of Shakespeare. I did my research, and my adolescent grandson enjoyed those CDs boom-booming over my car speakers, although his parents chastised me for exposing him to "crap music."

So here I was starting my second year of the Shakespeare program in the SHU—and facing a happy dilemma. The prisoners who had finished the first play did not want to leave the program, while the waiting list was growing each day. Should we serve a smaller number of prisoners for a longer period of time, or do we serve a larger number for a shorter time? Over the next eight years, I would experiment with both approaches, but for now, I opted to keep the dedicated core that I had, while adding a few enthusiastic newbies.

The second full play the prisoners read was *Hamlet*, twice as long and twice as difficult as *Macbeth*. If *Macbeth* hooked them in with its fast-paced and familiar criminal story, then *Hamlet* forced them to make their way through long, wordy speeches and ponder some sophisticated questions regarding the meaning of life. As if that weren't challenge enough, Newton was raising the bar in another, new direction.

After one year of exceptional performance in the program, through the individual work he did in his cell—and, not coincidentally, a year without any conduct infractions—Newton earned the right to come out of his cell and join the group discussions. It was a bit of a shock to see him for the first time without the pegboard door in front of him, and to see him actually walking down the hall, albeit on a leash and flanked by two officers. When they placed him in the individual cell, he dutifully turned and offered his hands to be uncuffed. I was struck by his quiet and respectful demeanor in his interaction with the officers. I found it hard to picture him in a violent rage, beating and stabbing Sgt. Harper—who was still, by the way, working in the SHU.

"This feels weird," he said, peering out through the little cuff port, looking around at the other faces in the cuff ports across from him. The others were already engaged in informal conversation. "I ain't scared," he said to me, and I suddenly realized that he was.

But from the start, he distinguished himself as an extraordinary member of the group. As impressed as I was with his written work, I was now equally impressed with his participation in the group. Without formal education, he was somehow able to excel in reading Shakespeare. And despite so many years without human interaction, he was somehow able to excel in teamwork. He raised challenging questions, but in such an informal manner that he never offended or intimidated his classmates. Instead, he got the best work out of them, like a good professor would. Additionally, he was able to speak with anyone, and even to diffuse tensions among other prisoners who could not get along.

Weekly arguments between a black man and a white supremacist in our group had often come close to getting out of hand. Newton was able to recognize when that was a risk and knew how to refocus them.

When he had been approved to join the group, he told me that he thought that we could use the plays of Shakespeare to encourage prisoners to examine their own lives: "The hope is that the more insight you get into these characters, the more insight you get into yourself," he told me excitedly. "That's what happened to me: I'm questioning why Macbeth does what he does, and I start to question why I do what I do. And I know I can re-create that experience for other prisoners. I *know* it, man!"

"Go ahead," I told him. "Try it."

As Hamlet says, "The readiness is all." Now that the group was assembled for their first discussion of their new play, it was time for Newton to try it. I was skeptical, and more than a little worried that his first session in the group would result in a unanimous rejection of his lofty ideal. But I didn't say a word. I wanted it to be their program.

"Hamlet is windier than a bag of farts!" said Green as the group session began.

The others laughed.

"Yeah, man, I agree," said Newton good-naturedly. And then he threw out his curveball: "But why do you think he's seeking revenge?"

I held my breath. The group did not outright reject his question, but no one, not even Green, had an answer. This group consisted of seven men who were serving murder convictions; the eighth was convicted of attempted murder. To these prisoners, it was a no-brainer: murder requires revenge, and revenge requires murder. Duh!

"This guy killed his father, so Hamlet should kill him?" Newton prompted them.

"That's right!"

"Sure!"

"That's what you do!"

"So, what? It's the 'honorable' thing to do?" he nudged them a bit more.

"Hell, yeah, it's honorable!" said Bentley, taking the bait.

"But why is it honorable?" he challenged them now. "What makes it honorable? And what *is* honor anyways?"

The group went quiet, thinking. No one had ever asked them to question such fundamental concepts that drove their lives and motivated their criminal choices. No one, that is, until Shakespeare—and Newton. Through the cuff port, he turned to me and gave me a wink. I nodded. We both knew that the Shakespeare program was entering a whole new dimension. We were going to be changing lives back here.

Chapter 29

Sensory Deprivation

Like other supermax units across the country, the SHU was designed as a unit of sensory deprivation. More than sixty such facilities currently exist, housing thousands of prisoners. However, decades of research have amply demonstrated the adverse effects of this kind of incarceration: hallucination, paranoia, rage, social isolation, and cognitive impairment among them. "Lengthy confinement in these facilities threatens prisoners' physical and mental health," concluded the Human Rights Watch in a published study titled *Cold Storage: Super-Maximum Security Confinement in Indiana.*

It's not that there are no senses engaged, but the sensations are monotonous: the same few voices you hear across the range every day, the same gray concrete walls. Those who are lucky enough to have a TV say that, over time, staring at the same programs day after day becomes every bit as monotonous as staring at the gray walls. The only human touch is the cold steel of the handcuffs and leg chains placed on you by the officers. Even the meals are required, by law, to be bland. Forget about spices; any identifiable flavors are prohibited.

During my training period, the chaplain, Father Bob, insisted that I have the full SHU experience and walked me into the inmate kitchen and handed me a tray with a pile of something mushy and gray. I had no idea what I was eating, and I complained to him the following week that it had made me sick.

"I eat it all the time," he said. "How come I don't get sick?"

I replied, "Father, you must be blessed."

I asked Newton to give me an example for each of the five senses that he was most aware of in the SHU. We started with the one that was most prominent: sound.

"*Chink-chink! Chink-chink!*" he said, imitating the sound of the officers snapping their handcuffs open and closed. "Man, they just sit out there by the pod doing that all day long. You can hear it all the way out onto the range. I actually thought they were trained to do that. Even over all the psych patients beating and banging all night, the thing that stands out most in my mind is the sound of them clicking the cuffs."

Smell.

"Poop," he said immediately, then added, "but you can smell rain, even worms. And I can hear it too, 'cause of the plastic on the top of the ranges. These are things that I love, but back here, everything becomes miserable. I love the smell of rain, but back here, it stinks. I love the sound of the rain, but in that miserable state, you find reason to make it evil. The idea of rain is pretty, but when you're miserable like that, you give it a violent association. Even things you like, you'll find ways to make it miserable."

Touch.

"Hot or cold. Never warm. Never comfortable. Always one extreme or the other."

Taste.

"The food, man! Yeah, it's bad, but it's more that that's where the focus of all that helplessness goes to. I think it's the sense of powerlessness that you associate to the food, the lack of any choice whatsoever."

Sight.

He laughed. "Just a bunch of little holes."

That one surprised me. I asked, "The pegboard door? Looking out, as opposed to looking in?"

"Absolutely, man! It's just another wall, but there's a space between those walls. There's a hallway, there's a door. You know, psychologically, that's how people travel. The hallway goes somewhere, always. I've counted the holes in the door, every one, I swear. Where else you gonna look? There's nothing to look at in the cell. You know, in my earlier years in the SHU—"

"Meaning, before Shakespeare?"

"Right," he said. "In those years, I always kept my light out. Most guys back here do."

"Why?"

"Ah, man," he said. "It's just such a dark place."

Then he added, "Let me tell you this about the SHU: You feel like you're decaying back here. You feel like you're melting away. You're just dying. You feel like you're going further and further into the grave! There's no kind of...*life* back here. It's, it's, just, man, a weird experience."

It was true. I noticed that when I walked the ranges, even in the middle of the day, I found most of the cells dark.

"But now," Newton continued, "I prefer the light on. And when I do turn the light on, I feel more prepped, like something's going on. I can work better. I have more energy."

"It's like sunshine: your day is beginning, regardless of what time it really is."

"Right. My body is saying, 'Get up, it's time to work.' But as soon as the range door opens, I turn it off."

"The range door opens and you know that someone is entering the range. But why do you want to go dark?"

"It's such a draining and dark environment, you just want

to blend into your environment. It's more comforting even though it's miserable. Does that make sense?"

"So you create your own 'dark cell' experience, in a way."

"You know, the dark didn't never bother me. I don't think anything bothered me as much as—let's see, what would've bothered me most of my whole isolated experiences? Probably just that real depressing sense of...loneliness."

Solitary confinement is inherently lonely, but in Newton's case, the experience was greatly exacerbated by his choice of silence over human contact.

Chapter 30

Isolated...and Alone

Of all of the thousands of prisoners I have worked with over the past quarter century, Newton has survived the most extreme experiences that I have ever heard of, from his hard-core home life to his supermax prison life. What he told me next seems impossible and probably would be, for anyone else.

"Have you ever been on a solo range?" I asked him.

"I've been on a range by myself, yeah."

"For how long?"

"I don't know, maybe a month or so."

"A *month* of no one to talk to?" I couldn't imagine it. I couldn't do it. I couldn't do a day—I don't think I ever have (even when I had laryngitis).

"Yeah," he said, "but I went a couple of *years* not talking to nobody at all."

I was stunned. That couldn't be physically possible. Could it?

"I didn't see any of my family for years, three or four years. It's understandable; I was such a down and nasty guy, all I would talk about is how miserable I was. And I didn't really relate with the guys around, even though we shared similar circumstances and maybe even similar experiences, but the discussions with them just made you feel worse: same conversations every day, no joke. Guys argued, same argument every day. Everything was so monotonous."

That explained why it happened, but I wanted to know how it happened, so I asked him, "What was that like?"

"Uh, let me see if I can remember." He thought for a bit. "Okay, the initial stage, I don't know what *ostracism* feels like, but I would guess that you kind of feel that way."

"Outcast?" I asked. "Or maybe out of place?"

"Right!" he said. "Exactly! Even though you're the one intentionally not talking, you feel like you don't fit in, don't belong. You just really feel—that's exactly right: out of place, initially. But that's not long, that's not long. That's just the very initial stage and then after that, I kind of found pleasure in it. I found things that I liked about not interacting with anybody. And this is a bad way to say it, but it gave me some form of like, supremacy, that I'm of a different league, you know? And I think that gave me little bit more confidence, a little bit more swagger, to be able to deal with the circumstances like that. But the initial stage, you're just this close to just pulling someone in a conversation. You hear something like, 'Hey! You know how to do fractions?' And you just wanna, 'Yeah! It's three over four!' You're just kind of desperate, you know what I mean?"

"Because you know the answer, or because you want to speak?"

"'Cause you just want to interact, you want to be involved, be noticed, or something."

"So why didn't you?"

"I think that I had just developed so much hatred for everything and everybody that it just bled out to those around me too. Some of them guys I could look back now and see he was a good dude. He coulda been talking positive things, but I would hate him: 'Aw, that dude's so fake, man!' I'd have these conversations with myself: 'That dude's a phony!' So I wouldn't talk, but when you hear a conversation, I don't care how tough you are, you take off your headphones and you listen, and you go through these dialogues with yourself: what you would say, how you would tear down his argument." He laughed. "You're kinda living like old Richard said, you know? Your whole world that you made all these characters right there in your head. I really was just so bitter and mad, and I never knew why. So if you don't know why, you just attach it to the easiest targets, and the guys around me were the easy targets. I just hated them. I'm sure internally I was just hating myself, but who can come to grips with that: 'I hate myself'?"

"So you just made a decision one day, or was it a gradual development?"

"Both. 'Cause, you know, that ain't the only time I've done that. I can remember making that decision: 'Yeah, I'm not talking to none of them cats, nobody, I'm not talking to nobody!' And other times that just being a consequence of being around these people: 'I ain't got nothing in common with them; what am I gonna talk about?' Michigan City, man, it's a whole different world, very much segregated, racially I mean. In lockup, there were only two white dudes, and I didn't relate to the other one. I mean, he'd bang Elavil and—"

"What?"

"Oh yeah," he laughed. "I forgot you're not a prisoner. 'Banging' is when you inject drugs, so he would take Elavil— it's an antidepressant drug, it's not a drug you bang, but he's such a dopehead that we didn't have a lot in common. So there wasn't nobody to talk to."

"I can't imagine it," I told him.

"It never really bothered me," he replied. "It didn't bother me not talking. It's only when you're used to talking and then you go to not talking, that initial probably couple of weeks of adjusting, and then you just learn to enjoy the solitude, being to yourself. And the same thing the other way, you just learn to enjoy talking to people again. So it's the same adjustment either way, the same awkwardness. I think I can handle both: I can handle the social, and I can handle the solitude."

It occurred to me that this was one of the few decisions that a segregated prisoner could make: to talk or not to talk. For Newton, that was the question.

"In the ten years that you spent in isolation, how many face-to-face conversations did you have?"

"*Man!*"

There was a long pause. Apparently, he couldn't think of a single one. Again, I was stunned.

"There was a behavior clinician that come through every month, does that count?" he said at last. "And I'd just say, 'Everything's fine.' 'Everything?' 'Everything.' Every time, that's what I'd say."

"Exactly those words?"

"Exactly those words."

"Every month?"

"Every month."

"Was it true?"

"No."

Chapter 31

Ghosts in the Cell

O God, I could be bounded in a nut shell
and count myself a king of infinite space,
were it not that I have bad dreams.

—*Hamlet*, act 2, scene 2

Supermax prisoners know how Hamlet feels being "bounded in a nut shell" and having "bad dreams." They also have a unique perspective on Hamlet's vision of the so-called ghost of his dead father that urges him to seek revenge for his murder by committing murder himself. I say "so-called" because the prisoners convinced me that the ghost could be—probably is—in Hamlet's mind, urging him to kill the uncle he hates. If you've read the play, you may question the fact that it opens with two nervous guards on patrol who think they have seen the ghost, and they then tell Hamlet's friend Horatio, who also comes to believe he has seen the ghost. The prisoners had a ready answer for that too:

"How many people have seen Elvis? Or Jesus?"

"Mass hysteria: they see what they need to see."

Makes sense. Once again, they were basing their interpretations on a detailed analysis of a passage that is often overlooked in classroom study, and nearly always cut in performances.

Furthermore, they know what it's like to see someone you really want to see. They have had their share of "ghosts" in their cells. Every one of them told me that he's had the experience.

"Any slight little shift in your head, it'll look like movement, that little break in the light through the cell door, so it's easy to get tricked into thinking somebody walked by your cell," Newton explained. "I could've swore at times there was someone in my cell, but it was me pumping myself into it, and wanting it so bad, interacting with a ghost."

"Did you see anyone in particular?"

"It's Aunt Jane!" He laughed. "No, man, I'd have to be crazy."

Wondering if he ever was on the brink of going crazy, I asked Newton to tell me more about the "fantastical walks" he had described earlier. In researching the psychological effects of supermax incarceration, I learned that a key distinction between sane fantasies and insane hallucinations is whether the prisoner believes the vision is real.

"How does it work?" I asked. "The fantastical walk."

"You start pacing," he said, and he started to do so, as if to demonstrate. "At first you're just thinking, about anything, and that evolves into thinking about life outside of the cell, on the streets. It's you somewhere else—it starts out with you in your past, hanging out on the streets with your guys, you at a party, then it's you at that party but how you would act now, with your mentality and personality now. The next stage is you're who you are now, but you're in a different life. You're fighting off all these other thoughts and distractions, so you don't get far." He stopped pacing and came back to the cell door. "It can take a week of ten-hour days of pacing to live three hours of a fantasy."

"Are you always aware that it's just a fantasy?"

"I think you're conscious of it as it goes. There's just certain defenses that you drop. The only way to appreciate the true feeling of those moments is to not make yourself aware that it's just a fantasy, 'cause that's distracting. You can't get 100 percent in it, but you want to get in as much as possible. You can get it to where you can feel the sensations, smell the food, feel the dampness of the rain."

"The power of the mind."

"Right. You can trick your mind to feel certain things. There's a feeling to all this, man, there's some kind of liberty, and if you just pick up where you left off, you lose that liberating feeling, so each time you start over, you rewalk into the house, whatever it takes to start again."

"It always starts with an entrance?"

"Right, exactly! I'm sure that has to do with that whole wanting to make an impression. I would play out these fantasies as I walked, but I would also play them out physically. Like, if I walk in the house, and I go sit down on a chair, I'll sit on the bed and act like I'm right across from the person I'm talking to. Like, 'Yeah, man, you know.' I'd do this whole gesture, and I'd do that with anything that I was doing in the fantasy."

"You'd get even more involved? For example, if you were playing cards, you would—"

"You would, right! You'd beat the desk, like 'Hey, what's up, man!' You'd physically do things, you're more involved, and that makes it more real."

"Did you one day make the decision to begin acting out the fantasies?"

"No! It was a natural development; it just started happening."

"When?"

"I don't remember doing that as much at WCU [Westville Control Unit, Indiana's other supermax] as in the SHU. So I don't know if it takes a certain amount of time of this kind of solitude, but where it got full-fledged was in the SHU."

"Do you talk?"

"Yeah, there is talking. If I sit down to drive: 'Hey, what's up, man?'"

"Do others speak?"

He laughed. "Yeah, but that part's in your head. You don't go, 'Hey, what's up?' and then respond, 'Not much, man.' You're the only vocal character. The other one's in your head."

"What comes first: speaking or gestures?"

"Gestures."

"How long after is speaking?"

"Not long after. Initial speaking is just gonna follow the gesture. You turn your head: 'Hey, what's up, man?'"

"Longer speeches too?"

"Later on, you will. Whole speeches, and then you gotta stop and restructure your speech, 'cause you're always trying to improve it. Your impact on the world. But if you ask a guy who's at the two-month stage about this three-year stage: 'That's retarded, man! Who does that? Freakin' psych patients!'"

"What gets you out of the fantasy is some kind of interruption?"

"It's not always external. Sometimes it's your own thought. Sometimes, you want to see what another fantasy is like."

"You switch channels?"

"You switch channels, that's exactly right! Now you're grown up, rich, doing these charitable things."

"Have you ever had difficulty getting out of a fantasy?"

"Well, that's one of them questions: How would I know? There were times that I worried about where my sanity was and how far I had gone. You don't know where the line is, so how do you know if you crossed it?"

It's the same question that has often been raised of Hamlet.

CHAPTER 32
Insanity

Hamlet fakes his insanity as part of his strategy to seek revenge on his uncle, while Newton was all too familiar with the real thing.

"Over the years, I've watched a lot of people go through psychological breakdowns back here," he told me, "and I got to know the symptoms."

"What are they?"

"It starts with the pacing. That's the initial stage that this place is starting to affect you. Then there's the desperation to talk, to anyone. That's the stage where it's starting to hurt you, you're starting to really want out of here, you're starting to tread water, or more like quicksand: if you stay calm, you'll be okay, but if you panic, you start sinking faster and faster. So the danger in that is that you do jump feetfirst into that SHU lifestyle: 'I'll throw poop on you!' That kind of outburst is so common back here. But I understand why they do that; there's passion in that kind of anger, there's a purpose in life."

"What happens later?"

"You develop that sense of powerlessness that you feel in a lot of situations, but after your fair share of seg time, it's much more prominent. You really feel like there's nothing you can do. A prisoner may not have a great deal of power, but early on, psychologically, he does feel he still has an outlet, a say in what goes on in his life."

"One short-term guy in the group today was complaining about his laundry being late."

"Yeah, you feel you have some say. You still feel you have some power."

"Short-term guys are not feeling long-term effects."

"Right, they still feel they have some power or say in their life. But later on—and I don't know if it's gender specific, but I've always felt that a guy has these impulses to be the provider, so the helplessness is hard to swallow, to think you can't take care of yourself. You want to feel like you can do these necessities, can take care of your family, of yourself. In seg, after so long, you get this sense of helplessness: there's nothing you control in your life, *nothing*! You need somebody else for everything in your life: for your clothes to be clean, for something to eat, to go to the shower, you need somebody else. After long exposure to that, it just grows into you and then you don't have any kind of confidence in yourself, you feel like that's your life, you feel like you're just this animal that they say you are."

"Do you ever come to accept the powerlessness?"

"To the breaking point, you're still fighting it, still searching for avenues and outlets to find power in. Shakespeare is one of them: a positive outlet, a source of power. In seg, there's a lot of bitterness and anger, and a lot of guys find those outlets in each other: fighting and feuding, arguing, having poop wars. But a guy like me, who didn't talk, didn't expose my hand to anybody, where could I find that outlet? 'I'm gonna kill you! Somebody's gonna pay!' And you have to ask, why does a guy do these violent acts? Psychologically, it's a sense of power he has over people. In these kind of conditions, where a guy's dealing with this whole power failure, having nothing to have power over, he can find a lot of power in that: killing people. Absolute power, you know?"

"So there are two outlets for the frustration of that powerlessness: insanity or violence."

"Right."

"How did you retain your sanity in segregation?"

"When people ask me, 'How did you stay sane all that time in seg?' I just say, 'You do what you gotta do.' People say, 'I think I'd go crazy,' and I say, 'You don't know what you're capable of.' That's what I say, but in my head, I attribute a lot of that to that..."

"That what?"

"The 'fantastical walks,' that I was able to leave, in a way, and live a different life while all this crap and turmoil was going on around me. And I think King Richard even mentions that. Doesn't he suggest that it's a coping mechanism?"

"So Shakespeare not only had the insight to know that's what you do in isolation, but also maybe even to know that it's the key to surviving?"

"Right—but, oh! Here's the thing, man: too much of a good thing can be bad. Because I had done this for a matter of years, right? You keep doing it over and over, and getting more involved to where you lose that reality line, and I thought about that: This must be how people do it, these people that really think and feel they're in different places or different people. They just get into these characters every now and then, and eventually they're not sure which one is real, and then they become this other. I remember thinking, 'This must be how it works.' And then obviously, the natural thing is to think: Where am I at? And when will I know? You don't know. You don't know what line to cross or not to cross. So, finally, it got to the point where as soon as I started doing the fantastical walk, my mind would start attacking, like 'That's retarded! What are you doing?' It would ruin it, I couldn't do it, and I remember hating that. Once my mind would go 'that's ridiculous,' I'd go 'damn!' because I really wanted to do it."

"When did you start fighting it?"

"Shakespeare did that to me too!"

"I wasn't thinking Shakespeare."

"Actually, I was. Because it's my investigation of Shakespeare's characters bleeding over into myself. You start asking questions of yourself: 'Why are you doing this?' It definitely came during my Shakespeare experience."

"But if it kept you sane—?"

"Why would you defend against it?" he asked, anticipating my question.

"Right."

"You start using it too much, you start getting addicted. I wanted to do it more and more. Instead of an hour, it got to where I was spending six, seven hours a day! And I did start to question my sanity."

"Did you lose touch with details of your identity, like your age?"

"I knew I was born in '76; I didn't lose that part. But I didn't necessarily know what year it was. I remembered that my birthday was November 9, but I didn't necessarily know what day it was. And then if I figured out that it was my birthday, it would bring on the question: How old am I?"

"How did you celebrate your birthdays?"

"I didn't celebrate at all. In a strange way, every year was kinda worrisome, 'cause I thought, 'Oh, man, that's one more year, I'm losing time!' I was still a kid, but I really felt that pressure: 'I'm running out of time!'"

Newton was just a kid, aged nineteen, when he entered supermax. And he wouldn't get out of that box until he was a thirty-year-old man.

Chapter 33

More House Calls

One late-summer Friday night I arrived at the SHU to find the unit manager, Ken Gilchrist, still in his office. Because my sessions took place in the evenings, the administrative offices typically were dark and empty during my time in the unit. Usually, I was the only one there.

"This can't be good," I said, trying to force my usual cheery voice.

"It's not," he replied, not as cheerily. "We intercepted a message indicating that one of your guys"—one of the largest prisoners in the unit, with a history of instigating prison riots—"is planning an assault on staff tonight."

I wondered if the prisoners considered me "staff." Apparently, the administration did.

"Does that mean that I can't have him in the group tonight?" (Is that a stupid question, or what?)

"No," he replied. "You can have him." I was surprised, and rather pleased that he trusted me enough to share the information and leave me alone. As he headed out of the unit, he added, "Just don't get too close to him."

"You mean physically, right?"

He turned back and looked at me. "Right."

After he left, I ran off copies of the day's assignment on

the unit's photocopy machine, collated the pages, opened up my vitaminwater, and headed down the long hallway toward the sally port that leads into the unit. First I stopped at the unit mailboxes. Under boxes labeled "Unit Team Manager," "Casework Manager," "Lieutenant," and others was a box labeled "Shakespeare." I reached inside: four more requests to join the program. At the end of the hallway, I pushed the intercom button and announced myself: "Shakespeare!" After another set of steel double doors rolled open and shut behind me, I entered the officers' sealed-off glass-enclosed pod, the central control unit. The lieutenant and his staff were focused on their computer screen, apparently monitoring activity in one of the cells on their closed-circuit television monitor. I gave them a cheery greeting, but immediately I could tell that they were not happy to see me.

"You can't have your group today," the lieutenant informed me, without turning around.

"Gilchrist told me about Jones," I said (not his real name). "He told me I could have him as long as I don't get too close to him."

"Can't have Jones," said the lieutenant. Then, turning to face me, he added, "And can't have your group."

"We're all worried about him," said one of the officers, a female. "What he might do."

"Well, what if I'm with you?" I offered. I was not suggesting that I could protect an officer better than he (or she) can protect me, of course, only that it's possible that the prisoner might not try an assault with a volunteer present.

"It's you that we're worried about," said the officer. "What he might do to *you*."

"Oh." It was looking like I'd have to make some more house calls to pick up homework and pass out next week's assignment. "Well, then, can I go out and talk to him at his cell?"

The officers looked at one another. The lieutenant shrugged, "If you want to."

"No group tonight?" said Bentley when I arrived at his cell. "Damn! I had some good questions." He handed me his homework. "Guess we'll have to discuss 'em on the range."

The others were equally disappointed, but when I arrived at Jones's cell, he was sitting on his bunk, angry. He wouldn't even come to the door.

"It's bullshit!" he shouted at me. (As I mentioned earlier, cussing in front of the Shakespeare professor was not common. It was, in this case, an indication of how angry Jones was.) "Come on, you know me, you know it's bullshit! Tell 'em! Tell 'em it's bullshit!"

"Obviously, Mr. Jones," I replied, "you are mistaking me for someone with power. What I think or say doesn't carry any weight around here, you know that. Now here's the assignment for next week."

I opened the cuff port and showed him the paper. He still wouldn't get off the bunk. I waved the paper at him and stood there. Eventually, he shuffled to the door, took the paper out of my hand, and gave me his homework. As he turned away he muttered again, "Bullshit."

The last member of the group I visited was Newton.

"Oh, hey, Dr. Bates!" he called out to me as soon as I stepped onto the range. "I'm in the shower."

SHU prisoners had no control over when they were brought into the shower, and the officers didn't take the Shakespeare sessions into account, I'm sure, when they scheduled the prisoners' showers.

"My paper's in the cell," Newton called out through the pegboard door of the shower cell. (I made a point of not looking in his direction.) "Door's open."

I walked in. It was my first time inside a segregation cell. It felt claustrophobic. I tried to imagine what it would feel like if the door suddenly rolled closed. I shuddered.

The light was on; the Shakespeare book was laid open on the bunk. I looked around for the paper. I took those five steps that Newton's walked a million times, from the door to the bunk: one…two…three…four…five.

I saw the paper on the steel platform that serves as a writing desk. I picked it up and stepped toward the door: one…two…three…four…five…

Six. I exited the cell with a sense of relief.

"See you next week!" I called out in the direction of the shower as I left the range.

Chapter 34

Administrative Segregation versus Disciplinary Segregation

Newton was dressed in bright orange scrubs when he came to the group, but most of the others were in more subdued khakis. Eventually, I learned about the difference between A/S versus D/S, or Administrative Segregation versus Disciplinary Segregation. The two supermax units in the state designate a prisoner under one of these two distinctions. A prisoner who is considered a potential risk, perhaps due to alleged association with a gang, will be designated A/S. Because he is not being punished for a conduct infraction, he has many of the same privileges that prisoners in general population have, while enjoying the "luxury" of a private cell. Prisoners who voluntarily "check in" are also in this category; they have requested long-term segregation because they fear for their lives in general population. Prison snitches and child molesters are two common examples of check-ins.

D/S is altogether different: a much harsher and more restrictive environment. It is never the original crime that sends a prisoner to supermax with a D/S designation; it is his conduct while incarcerated. Prisoners who have accumulated more than two years of segregation due to serious conduct infractions are sent to supermax for D/S. At one point in his segregated term, Newton had more than fifteen years of D/S time accumulated. Through good behavior, beginning with the Shakespeare program, he ended up serving "only" ten years in solitary confinement.

"I did ten years of D/S—straight! No break!" he emphasized. "Don't be thinking I was on A/S living the cushy life."

He was being ironic, of course, in referring to any kind of life in segregation as "cushy," but I got the point: it's one thing to have survived ten years of A/S; entirely another to have survived ten years of D/S.

"One of the hardest things about D/S," he told me, "is there's no liberty whatsoever. *None.* You can't just order food off commissary for a snack, you starve all night, you gotta bear it till breakfast, you gotta eat every piece of crap. When you have food, like the A/S guys, you just have more options. To someone on the outside looking in, that's just ridiculous, but that's a huge difference in lifestyle. Food is…liberty."

Granted, the conditions in any kind of long-term solitary confinement cell are tough, but they have also been earned. I want to be clear that I do not consider myself a "prisoner advocate" in that I am not crying over their conditions. And neither was Newton. One of his most common philosophical expressions applied here: "It is what it is."

Although they were committed many years ago, offenses such as attempted escape and assault had earned him a lengthy term in segregation. But Newton's last violent incident occurred during the escape attempt of May 2000. Should he spend the rest of his life in segregation?

CHAPTER 35

Killer Dog

Is rehabilitation possible? This topic came up one day when we were talking about his past behaviors, and Newton said, "I think I was like a killer dog, just aimlessly 'Raa! Raa! Raa!'"

The metaphor seemed apt—and led to the idea of rehabilitation.

"But here's the thing, man," he continued. "There are people that work dogs like that, rehabilitate 'em, so they ain't got to be euthanized."

I saw a metaphorical parallel to Newton's not being euthanized on death row and to the possibility of his rehabilitation.

"That doesn't mean that the dog would never bite somebody," Newton acknowledged. "As long as this dog has teeth there's no way to guarantee that he's never gonna bite somebody. But the circumstances for why the dog bites are different. If he's backed into a corner, he might bite someone, but he doesn't *want* to bite. He's not walking around looking for someone to bite. His motivation in life is different. It's all the way different!"

It was a serious topic, but I had to chuckle at the idea of a dog's motivation in life. (A few biscuits and a scratch under the chin, perhaps?)

"But how can you tell somebody this and successfully convince them?" he asked. "If all I know is that this used to be a rabid dog and now you're telling me that he's a peaceful, cool dog, it's gonna be hard for me to absorb that. He used to be rabid so he could still be rabid; that's what's gonna attach to my mind. Because there's the danger."

And there's the challenge for me, in writing up his life story and the story of our program.

"But if it's true," he continued, "if this killer dog really is a peaceful kind of dog now and he won't revert back to the rabid dog, then that's amazing. That's awesome. That is just the greatest thing ever. What a dog!"

Yes, what a dog! This is not just a rehabilitated dog lying down passively; this is a dog who is actively rehabilitating other killer dogs. That's what Newton was doing in his approach to *Hamlet*. As the acknowledged leader of the group by now, he threw out another challenge. In his most daring move, he insisted that in the group's creative adaptation of the play they change the ending. In their version, with the title "To Revenge or Not to Revenge," Hamlet should choose *not* to kill.

Chapter 36
Extraction

One day as I was about to enter one of the ranges, I heard a sudden commotion behind me. Before I could turn around, I was nearly knocked over by a team of officers running onto the range—as many as eight officers, most of them wearing body armor, helmets with visors, and heavy leather gloves, and carrying shields. It looked like some sort of medieval duel, only more frantic. I was about to witness my first extraction.

Extraction is the forcible removal of an inmate from his cell. The specially trained team consists of at least five officers, accompanied by a supervising sergeant, a video camera man, and a medical assistant. Each team member is assigned a body part to subdue and place in restraints: right arm, left arm, right leg, left leg, head. In its early years of operation, the SHU averaged several extractions per week.

Newton was involved in a group demonstration at WCU that had ended in a cell extraction of each of the prisoners involved. The hostage incident in the SHU was his second experience with forcible removal by an extraction team. By then he knew what to expect when the officers arrived at the range in which he and his accomplices had been sealed off following the stabbing of Sgt. Harper.

"They suit up and come and get you," he told me. "They come in with all this gear. It's really intimidating."

And then he described the conditions he endured after the SHU extraction.

"I'm not claiming the 'victim' issue," he said, "but this is no joke: I was stripped out for like sixteen days in my boxers, that was it. Sixteen days sitting like that on a strip cell."

A strip cell is an empty cell in which a prisoner sits in nothing but his underwear. I once got reprimanded for handing a prisoner in a strip cell a single sheet of paper (a Shakespeare speech).

"And they would bring me these sacks," he continued. "I didn't get trays. I'd get my meals in sacks. And they would spray OC into my sack. You know what OC is? That chemical they use [pepper spray]. Aw, man! That stuff's terrible! They would spray it in my little coffeecake sack, and it's not a hallucination, you know when your eyes start burning. Like, 'What the—!' And I don't go around making issues like, 'I got treated bad!' But the point is, what do you do? You buckle down and you freakin' eat it. For two reasons: on principle and you're hungry, you know what I mean? On principle, I'm not gonna let 'em win, I'm not gonna let 'em get to me."

It's understandable that the officers would harbor resentment against any prisoner who had attacked one of their own, and published reports such as *Cold Storage: Super-Maximum Security Confinement in Indiana* suggest that officers in the unit were more, to use Newton's term, "rowdy" in the past than they are today.

"They'd sit outside my cell and just stare at me all night," Newton recalled. "They had a midnight shift, they were rowdy and obnoxious and just thought they were untouchable, and they would come and stand outside the cell. Just stare at me. All night. I don't have no TV, I'm on a strip cell, I couldn't hide from it. I'd have to sit and just look at them, and I would, and they'd look away. I'm sure internally I was worried, nervous, all that kind of stuff. But I'd refuse to show any signs of break whatsoever. Not that I didn't want to, but just on principle, you know? Same thing with the food. So I would eat that out of spite. Like, 'Yeah, okay!' That stuff just eats you up. Everything burns in your face. But I would eat it. In those days, they had vindictive officers like that back there, no joke."

Based on my observations of the hardworking and well-intentioned officers during the ten years I worked at the SHU, it was clear to me that conditions improved a great deal since those days. But when he recalled his early experiences, Newton concluded: "I don't know, man, the SHU does something to you."

Following the hostage attempt, Newton was housed in B-East, the most notorious wing of the SHU. That experience certainly did something to him—it drove him to the brink of suicide.

Chapter 37

B-East

B-East, also known as Beast, was still the most notorious wing of the SHU when I started working there. Three ranges in particular housed the worst of the "worst of the worst." Most of the pegboard cell doors there were covered with clear plexiglass that was smeared with the bodily fluids that had been thrown by the desperate prisoner inside. When I tried to talk to a prisoner through that barrier, I wondered how he could breathe. "You just feel like you're suffocating back here," one prisoner said, "like you're always coming up for air."

Newton had spent more than his share of time in what was almost exclusively the insane ward of the SHU. Imagine the challenge of retaining your hold on sanity in long term isolation. Now imagine that all of the other prisoners around you are insane: not a single sane voice to hold on to. That was Newton's situation when he was held in B-East after the hostage attempt.

"That was the worst time ever," he told me, recalling the experience. "Worst time in my life! I was never as bad before that incident as I was after that incident. I was on B-East for like two years. It's only supposed to be ninety days but they kept me there, on Range Five, which was the worst range."

When I was in training with Father Bob, he never took me to B-East. It took me months of working in the SHU before I felt ready to venture onto those ranges. I did try to talk with a few of the inmates on B-East, but communication was all but impossible through those plexiglass partitions, and the inmates were too unfocused to comprehend, or to care about, anything Shakespearean.

"Did you ever see any human beings?" I asked Newton about his time in B-East.

"You see a lot of nurses, passing out meds all the time. And what's worse, you see a lot of extractions. That's where the strap-down beds were."

Strap-down beds were used to subdue unruly prisoners after a cell extraction; their hands and feet were bound to the bed with leather straps. The strap-down bed was located in cell 3. He was upstairs in 11, right above it.

"It was so infuriating! When you're bitter, it gives you something to attach that to. So there was no escape from that for me during that period: everywhere you turn it's all part of your misery."

In such relentless misery, it was easy to understand why prisoners did desperate things to try to escape their condition.

"When you're at the bottom, and there's no relief from the torment, you really feel trapped. I like to use the analogy that you're way out in the middle of the ocean. You're scared, panicking, desperate to do anything. You try swimming in one direction, you try another direction. You're just desperate; that's why you do desperate things and you overlook that it's gonna make it worse. You see the potential for land, not thinking that it's more sharks over there."

Again, the analogy seemed apt.

"But, *man*!" he said again, shaking his head at the thought. "That had to be the most miserable time in my life!"

"And that was just before—"

"That's right," he said, finishing my sentence. "Just before Shakespeare."

Chapter 38

This Prison Don't Matter

When the SHU group got back together again after the cancelled session the previous week, even Jones was allowed to participate. Newton led a discussion of Hamlet's observation that, to those who see it that way, all the world is a prison.

HAMLET: What have you, my good friends, deserved at the hands of fortune, that she sends you to prison hither?
GUILDENSTERN: Prison, my lord!
HAMLET: Denmark's a prison.
ROSENCRANTZ: Then is the world one.
HAMLET: A goodly one; in which there are many confines, wards and dungeons, Denmark being one o' the worst.
ROSENCRANTZ: We think not so, my lord.
HAMLET: Why, then, 'tis none to you; for there is nothing either good or bad, but thinking makes it so: to me it is a prison.

Naturally, the group related to Hamlet's feeling of imprisonment. It inspired some of them to complain about their conditions, others to discuss their attempts to get out: the appeals they have filed, the DNA evidence or the new witness that will exonerate them for sure.

"This prison don't matter," Newton countered. "It's not that you're in prison. I'm sure it doesn't help matters, but a lot of the guys here were in prison before they came here and they'll still be in prison when they leave here."

Once again, Newton threw out an idea that the group had not grappled with before. And it was an important concept for them.

"That's one of the problems I think a lot of people have," he continued. "They associate their misery to the fact that they're in prison, and it's not that. I think a lot of my misery was me hating me, and hating me made me hate everyone else. I felt like such a punk, I felt so weak. I really was a coward. I never stood up for myself. I mean, I stood up for myself as we associate standing up for yourself—fighting and violence. But that's not standing up for yourself. I mean standing up for myself like thinking for myself. Now, I feel more okay with myself. I'm feeling stronger in my abilities every day, and the world just opens up. You really can do anything, you can shape your life any way you want it to be. Because prison isn't the great prison. Prison is being entrapped by those self-destructive ways of thinking."

Chapter 39

Meeting of the Minds

For two years now, I had seen that Newton's insights into prison and prisoners were of great value to the prison population. I started feeling that his insights into Shakespeare could be of value to the academic world as well. I presented several professional papers on our work at national and international conferences. Some of these papers were published in collected volumes on Shakespeare studies. I was starting to earn an international reputation among Shakespeare scholars for this unusual and groundbreaking work. I was pleased that this would help me professionally, of course, but I was also pleased that it would provide a voice for the voiceless prisoners who motivated my work from the beginning.

I decided to share this work with my PhD dissertation director, Professor David Bevington. I considered him not only a great scholar, but also a great human being. He had traveled to a number of prisons in Chicago and Indiana to observe my work with Shakespeare and inmates, and he conducted guest lectures for my incarcerated students in the Indiana State University Correctional Education Program. When I presented him with the ultimate invitation—to travel three hundred miles to meet with a lifer in supermax—of course, he accepted.

Newton's enthusiasm for Shakespeare was becoming

contagious throughout the prison population. "You can catch Shakespeare like a bad bug," one prisoner told me, "and you just can't shake it." We received permission from the prison administration to begin circulating a weekly Shakespeare Newsletter, introducing more than two thousand maximum-security prisoners to the plays of Shakespeare. Each week, Newton read a play and wrote an introduction in his inimitable style: "Lions, and tigers, and bears, oh my!" began his *Macbeth* introduction. "To the moon, Alice!" was the opening of his *Taming of the Shrew* introduction. "Boy meets girl" described the basic plot of *Othello*. In each case, the uneducated incarcerated reader was not intimidated by the idea of looking into Shakespeare. On the contrary, Newton put the reader at ease—and then always threw out those curveballs: his challenging, life-altering questions.

And now here he was, sitting next to one of the world's leading Shakespeare scholars, about to engage in a unique meeting of the minds. He was bouncing his right leg nervously, and sweat was visibly accumulating on his brow—the nervousness undoubtedly enhanced by the fact that this conversation was being observed by the prison superintendent, the staff videographer, his Shakespeare professor and her husband, and Amy Scott-Douglass, an author of a book on studying Shakespeare in prison. Surrounded by these six people in this cramped space, he had to somehow focus his thoughts on the plays of Shakespeare. Furthermore, we had caught him off guard; he did not know that we were coming.

"Did Shakespeare write *King John* after experiencing the death of a child of his own?" That was Newton's opening question. "Because the grieving over the death of Arthur just seems so *real*, man."

Sitting at opposite ends of the little room, Amy and I exchanged glances and smiled. Newton had just opened with a perceptive insight into one of Shakespeare's most obscure plays.

He was already focused, and from the way he addressed Professor Bevington as "man," I knew that he was on a roll. I was equally impressed with Bevington, who seemed perfectly at ease with this convicted killer sitting beside him, as they leaned close to each other to look at the Shakespeare book together. Over the next hour, their conversation bounced freely through twelve different plays: *King John*, *Hamlet*, *King Lear*, *Julius Caesar*, *Henry the Fourth*, *Henry the Fifth*, *Henry the Sixth*, *Richard the Second*, *Richard the Third*, *Othello*, *Taming of the Shrew*, and, of course, *Macbeth*.

"I felt like I could relate to Macbeth," said Newton, "and I never exonerated him because of the influence of the witches. I mean, we all have influences."

Bevington nodded in agreement.

"But *Julius Caesar* has one my favorite freakin' quotes," he continued, quoting from memory: 'So every bondman in his own hand bears the power to cancel his captivity.' To me, that's empowering, that we can free ourselves at any time—psychologically, I mean."

With his dog-eared and annotated copy of *The Complete Works of Shakespeare* in front him, Newton was able to flip through the two thousand pages and find a particular quote he needed instantly, without even a pause in the conversation.

"I'm sorry, man," he interrupted the professor at one point, "but I just love this! I think it's the bottom line with bad deeds: it always takes more bad deeds to protect the first. And I've noticed that's a theme in a number of plays." He flipped through the book as he continued, "I don't think that's a common insight. I think it's awesome that Shakespeare had that insight." He found the quote while talking.

"'There is no sure foundation set on blood, no certain life achieved by others' death,'" he read from *King John*, act 4, scene 2. Then he slapped the book and added, "Exactly, exactly! That's our life in here, man!"

The lively dialogue continued until, eventually, two officers arrived at the door. The superintendent nodded. As the officers began to cuff and shackle Newton, he dutifully turned and offered his hands behind his back—but he was still talking Shakespeare.

"I think *Henry the Fifth* is my favorite play," he said as they began to walk him out. "What a guy! I really want to be like him: strong, confident…honorable."

Professor Bevington got up from the table to make room for the officers. As Newton was being cuffed, he shook his head in disbelief at the conversation that had just taken place.

"Amazing," he said to me. I nodded. I knew it was unlike any Shakespearean dialogue he'd ever had at the university.

Newton thanked the professor for his time before being escorted out of the room. As we watched him disappear down the long corridor, walking on a leash between two officers and clutching his Shakespeare book with his hands cuffed behind his back, Professor Bevington turned to me and repeated, "He's truly amazing."

Chapter 40
Dr. Newton

Soon after his meeting with Professor Bevington, Newton told me that he wanted to enroll in college classes when he was released into the general prison population. Furthermore, and despite the fact that he had not been in school since the fifth grade, he announced with a big grin: "I want to be the first prisoner in the state of Indiana to earn a PhD while incarcerated!"

That evening, I emailed Bevington the exciting news, and when I saw Newton the next week, I showed him the response that I received.

"I'm pleased indeed to hear about Newton," wrote Bevington. "I support the idea of his working toward the PhD. I do believe in him."

Newton was beaming.

"How about that?"

"That's cool, man! It's real cool!" Then he turned to me. "Hey, what about you?" he asked. "Did you ever get that 'tenancy' or whatever it is?"

He meant "tenure," which would not only earn me a promotion and a salary increase, but it would also mean a permanent position at the university—without which I would find myself instantly unemployed. It is the academic paradox: up or out. At any university, an assistant professor's first six years must be followed by application for tenure. With tenure comes promotion to the next rank: associate professor. But if the promotion committee feels that tenure has not been earned, through a strong record of teaching, service, and scholarship, that professor cannot be retained.

"I sure hope so," Newton said. "You deserve it, man!"

I didn't tell him, but my first application for tenure was rejected. Because of my years as a visiting assistant professor, I had been eligible for early tenure. My teaching reviews were good, and I knew that my prison work "counted" as community service, so I submitted the application hoping for the best. Unfortunately, I was lacking in the required number of publications in peer-reviewed academic journals. Admittedly, I had been too busy with my prison work to write them. My colleagues had warned me.

"But I'm using literature to change people's lives," I countered.

Committees don't care. They don't know prison; they know peer-reviewed academic publications—the more footnotes, the better.

And here's an irony: as a direct result of my work in prison, I was on probation myself.

Chapter 41

The Picture

"You're on the boat again, aren't you?" I asked.

"What am I *doing*?" Newton asks. "How do you always know?"

"When your mind loses focus, so do your eyes," I said. "And I know the boat is your liberty, but remember—"

"Shakespeare is my liberty," he finished my sentence. "That's true. And *you* are my liberty."

I didn't think he meant that in an inappropriate way, but to be sure, I said, "Not me, Shakespeare."

"Right, of course, I didn't mean—"

"Good."

"But hey! You know what? I…"

"You what?"

"I, uh, drew a picture the other day. My first drawing in years, man! Just from memory."

"That's good," I said.

"Of you," he added.

"That's bad."

"Why? I'm a good artist."

It's true; he is. Another remarkable accomplishment for a man who's spent most of his life in a box.

"A waste of your talent," I said.

"Says who? Who gets to make that call: the artist, or the subject?"

"You're always railing against being treated like a subject, and now you're turning me into a subject!"

We both laughed at the irony.

With some trepidation, I asked, "Well, can I see it?"

"No."

"Why not?"

"I don't have it anymore."

Oh, great. I started envisioning a porno portrait of his middle-aged Shakespeare professor—sunbathing nude on the deck of a boat, perhaps—circulating among the prisoners in the segregation unit. They've been locked away for a long time, but are they really that desperate?

"I sent it to my mom," Newton said, much to my surprise—and relief. "I wanted her to meet you."

According to prison regulations, volunteers cannot have any outside contact with prisoners' friends or relatives, but I often wondered what it would be like to sit down and have a chat over a cup of coffee with Mom. What would I learn about life with little Larry? Would she recall happy memories of his first Christmas? Or would she remember him as a holy terror?

He didn't shirk responsibility for driving his parents crazy with more than the usual adolescent misbehavior. Still, I knew from his medical records that the abuse had been extreme at times. I even wondered whether his mom might have suffered abuse herself. Certainly, her life has never been easy. Newton was proud of telling me that she took on two jobs when his stepdad became ill and couldn't work, because she never wanted to go on welfare. I respected her for that. (My mom had worked two jobs too.)

The following year, at the annual Shakespeare performance at the prison, I would meet Mom in person. Several years younger than me, she was only sixteen when Newton was born—and he was her second child. She struck me as a caring, hardworking woman who had done the best she could as a teenage single mother. Her other two sons, one older than Newton and the other younger, turned out all right. One is a minister and the other is a police officer—at the same university in Muncie where Christopher J. Coyle had been killed.

An example of Newton's artwork,
a drawing inspired by Shakespeare's Macbeth.

Chapter 42

"That's Freedom"

In the summer of 2006, after more than ten years in isolation, Newton received word that he would finally be released into the general prison population. That was the good news. The bad:

"They'll probably ship me back up to the City," he informed me, "'cause that's where I come from."

"The City" is Michigan City, one of only three maximum-security facilities in the state. It is, unfortunately, at the opposite end of the state. The day before his transfer date, we had one last group session. Later that same evening, I returned to the SHU for a private session with Newton—with the approval of the unit manager and the sergeant on duty. It was Harper, the sergeant Newton had stabbed six years ago.

"He's changed a lot," Harper said to me as his officers went to remove Newton from his cell. "If Shakespeare did that, then I'm impressed."

If you've read this far into this book, it should be clear to you that my relationship with Newton was never inappropriate in any way, least of all romantic; as I said, I am older than his mother. But like saying farewell to a colleague with whom you've worked intensely for years, this farewell was bittersweet: I was happy to see him being released from his cage, sad to think what the loss of him would mean to the Shakespeare program.

We sat alone in the R&R area, where we'd had so many lively and fruitful group sessions. It was eerily quiet without those voices now. Even the hallway seemed unusually quiet. It'd been three years since we met, but this was the first time we had sat down together alone, not in a group or at a cell door, but just sat together for a normal conversation—normal, that is, if you disregard the fact that one of us was sitting in a box and peering out through a little slot. We talked optimistically about Newton's future, including his determination to pursue that dream of a college education, even a PhD.

All too soon, our hour was up and the officers came to take Newton back to his cell. When he reached his hands out through the cuff port for the officers to put on his leash, he had a folded-up piece of paper between his fingers. One of the officers took it and looked it over. Then he handed it to me. I stuffed it in my pocket while I watched Newton being cuffed and chained for the last time.

How do you say good-bye forever without a hug, a handshake, or even a pat on the back? As I stood locked behind the steel and glass of the sally port on my way out of the unit, I could see him being led down the hall in chains. I gave him a thumbs-up and forced a smile. He responded with a wink and a smile that was, I thought, equally forced.

Whenever a participant left the program, I distributed a short survey in which I asked, "What has Shakespeare done for you?"

"It helped me to expand my mind," Green had written.

"It introduced me to a whole new world," Jones had written.

"It got me out of my cell," Guido had written.

After I watched Newton disappear down the hallway, I took the folded paper out of my pocket. It was the survey. What has Shakespeare done for you? He had written, "Shakespeare saved my life."

Shakespeare Saved My Life.

Chapter 43
Another Door Opens

Each week when I drove home from the prison, I came to an intersection where the highway crosses a small country road. I usually drove straight ahead, but that night, waiting for the light to turn green, I recalled Newton's words about freedom. I could go straight, as usual, or I could turn; either road would lead somewhere. That intriguing little road disappeared into a grove of trees. I'd always wondered where it might lead. That night, as I thought about the new roads that Newton would be exploring in his journey back into population, I turned.

When I got home, my husband poured me a glass of wine, toasted my accomplishments of the past three years, and commiserated with me over the loss of Newton. The next morning, he also shared my jubilation over the email that I received from the SHU unit manager: "Offender Newton was transferred today into F-house. Thought you'd like to know."

F-house! He was not sent to the other end of the state, after all; he was sent to the other side of the facility! Immediately, I requested permission for Newton to be admitted into the Shakespeare group in open population. I learned that a ninety-day period of "quarantine" was required when prisoners transitioned from segregation to population, during which they were not permitted to participate in any kind of programming, work, or school activities. This struck me as a good idea, and especially for a prisoner who had spent so many years isolated as Newton had.

That's why it came as a surprise when the SHU manager suggested that I take advantage of Newton's forced idle time to work with him—but I agreed, of course. And I suggested that we use the time to create a workbook for the Shakespeare program that could be used in the SHU, which would present segregated prisoners with Newton's insights and questions, even though he was no longer there in person. Even more remarkable, the manager obtained permission for me to meet with this hard-core prisoner—one just released after ten years in supermax—face-to-face, one-on-one, alone and unsupervised. Absolutely unprecedented.

Chapter 44

Killer Dog Comes Inside

I arrived at the prison the following week with a good deal of trepidation: Would Newton be able to handle the social contact after so many years of isolation? Would I be able to maintain my composure, or would my nervousness cause a similar response in him? And how well did I really know this prisoner? Could I trust him...with my life? Strangely, I felt the kind of anxiety that Newton had described feeling prior to the murder: "There is a point of no return," he said, "when you have to fully commit to the deed." That's where I was now.

"No way!" the officer on duty told me when I arrived at the appointed location for our first session. "You know who he is?" he asked his partner. "He's the one that stabbed the sergeant." He turned back to me and repeated, "No way I'm bringing *him* out!"

My method of dealing with administrative adversity had always been nonconfrontational, friendly, even self-effacing. It had always worked—until that night. I hit a brick wall. To make matters worse, I was stuck at the prison for the next five hours because my husband was teaching two back-to-back classes there himself that semester. Adding insult to injury, I was battling the flu and would rather have been home in bed than sitting for hours in a cold, empty prison classroom. But it was Friday night, and all of the administration officials who had approved my session were gone. Utterly defeated, the only thing I could think to do was return to my home base, the SHU.

"You can have anyone you want here," the officers offered. I smiled at the irony: two hundred prisoners in the most locked-down unit in the state were more accessible to me than one prisoner in open population.

"Who is it you need?" asked the sergeant on duty. It was Harper.

"Well, uh..." I hesitated. "Actually, it's Newton."

Harper picked up the phone, placed a call, then turned to me and said, "You're all set." As I walked away, he repeated, "He's changed a lot."

Coming to our first-ever individual Shakespeare session would be Newton's first free movement, unchained and unescorted, in more than ten years. The SHU manager had assured me that our first meeting would be supervised, held in the public visitation wing, but the officers on duty didn't want to be near him, so they put me in an empty classroom down the hall. I asked them if I could at least prop open the door to reduce the suspicion of trafficking or any kind of inappropriate behavior. I was thinking more of protecting Newton than me, since my conduct history has always been spotless, but the officers removed my little pad of paper from under the door and shut me in. If they were that afraid of him, how worried should I be? As I sat and waited for his arrival, I recalled his earlier comparison of himself to a killer dog.

"How do we know when the killer dog can come into the house?" I had asked him.

"You never do. It's still a dog, it's still got teeth, it can still bite. There's no line that lets you know it's a safe thing to do. But if you are the owner of the dog, you've developed a trust."

"Okay, so I'm the owner of this dog—"

"That's right. You *are* the owner of this dog. We have a relationship. You just know what you know—hopefully." He had laughed nervously. “Hopefully, you know. And then one day, you have to say, ‘I’m gonna let him in tonight.’ There has to be that first time, that barrier-breaking kind of time, with a little angst. You know, ‘Okay, come on in…’”

Just then, the door opened and he came in. He looked around; he looked nervous. It was our barrier-breaking time.

Later, he would describe for me the moment when his cell-house door rolled open and he stepped into the open evening air—alone. He just stood there, in the doorway. The prison yard was overwhelming, full of inmates walking past, running on the track, or playing basketball on one of several courts. He looked to his left and to his right. A few officers were standing in front of the cell house, joking with one another while keeping an eye on the yard. He told me he felt awkward having to go up to them and ask where he should go, since he was not at all familiar with the prison yard and the layout of the buildings surrounding it. One of the officers pointed across the yard to a small building that housed the visitation room. As he walked away, he felt that their laughter was directed at him. He was so self-conscious walking across the yard that he felt like everyone was looking at him, as if a spotlight was on him. It seemed like the longest walk ever! He told me that he felt “exposed and vulnerable”—and that when he entered the building and saw me, he felt “safe.”

I watched him as he approached the window where the officer on duty checked him in behind the glassed-in pod. I saw him leaning down to speak directly into the microphone.

“Newton,” I heard him state his name and then his number. “Ninety-one, forty-three, eighty-two. Yes, sir. Thank you, sir.”

I walked over to him and reached out my hand. He hesitated a minute, not understanding what I wanted. I took his hand in mine, shook it, and, for the first time, called him by his first name.

“Welcome to the world, Larry.”

Chapter 45

"Shakespearean Considerations"

Each week, Larry came to our sessions with a stack of pages he'd written for our first workbook, *Shakespearean Considerations: Connecting Literature to Life*. In his introduction, he encourages his fellow prisoners to accept the Shakespearean challenge: "Shakespeare offers us a challenge to connect his classic literature to our own lives today. Macbeth is no monster; he is more like us than he is different." And he reminds his readers that a wise man learns from others' mistakes.

But it's not as simple as those of us looking from the outside in would like to think.

"I know what you want to hear," Larry said to me, "that this guy, Macbeth, he went through hell because of what he did, so what I learned is not to do that because I don't want to suffer. But that's just the way it looks on paper. That's not the way it works in real life."

"How does it work?" I asked, feeling that he was on the brink of unlocking the key to the whole problem of criminal behavior that has plagued mankind forever.

"Well," he continued, thoughtfully, "we've been hearing that message all our lives: 'If you do this, then that will happen.'"

"Pronouns, Larry!" The English teacher in me reminded him to be more specific in his use of language. "What's 'this' and what's 'that'?"

"Murder," he replied, "and prison. If you kill, then you'll be locked away—for life. But that doesn't have the impact you want it to have. It's really hard to appreciate the consequences of your actions if you haven't experienced it."

"So what does work?" I asked.

"You have to find a way for the guy to *relate* to Macbeth. And then, when he's questioning Macbeth's motives, he starts to question his own. And then he comes to his own conclusions—and then, real change is possible."

I pointed to our workbook. "That's what we're doing here."

"That's right," he said, "that's what we're doing."

For each of the workbooks, he presented thirty challenging "considerations" that address such weighty topics as honor, revenge, remorse, and conscience. For example:

> *In act 1, Macbeth tells his wife that they will not be discussing the deed any more, that he is settled on the position he already has. Some people look at that as evidence that his conscience is having an effect on his resolve. So I would like you to consider the source of his changed mind—which, by the way, does not require much persuading to change back again. Is it his conscience? Look at his own words. He is not telling his wife that it is wrong, that it is evil, that you do not treat people you love this way, or anything of that nature. His concerns are what? One, getting caught: "If we should fail?" Two, what it will do to his reputation. He tells his wife that he has "bought golden opinions from all sorts of people" and that he should not throw that away so quickly. Every one of his concerns is about himself. His image. There is no concern for the life of King Duncan, or how wrong such a deed is. It is not our conscience that torments us over our image; that is our ego tormenting us. Our conscience torments us when we behave in ways that are contrary to our values. When you look in the mirror and cringe as a result of your shame, it is*

conscience. When you look in the mirror and cringe as a result of how people think of you, it is ego. Which of the two is more prevalent in your life?

"You know," he told me enthusiastically as we looked over the final draft of the workbook, "I got people in the cell house reading *Macbeth*, three different guys. They just begged me. They're not even in the education program. They do it 'cause they just want to check it out. That's kinda cool, I think. So I'm at work one day—"

Larry's job was working in the prison industries, making leather belts for the military. It was the first real job he'd ever had, and he proudly showed me his first check stub. It was not an easy adjustment into the "real world" of working full-time, while taking college classes at night…and leading a Shakespeare program.

"—and one of the guys, one of the other line bosses, he's on his machine, and I'm on my machine, and he says, 'Yeah, they just killed Duncan.' And I said, 'Why'd you say *they*?' I wanted to engage him in discussion, you know, deeper thought about it. And he's like, 'I mean Macbeth did, but Lady Macbeth, she pretty much made him do it.' And I said, 'That's probably the most popular argument, man. I'll wait till you finish before I try to tear it up for you.' It's cool, it's really cool. I mean, I know the program is doing something, I know it's going somewhere, but that was the first time it hit me: this really is gonna do something, it really might get to somebody. And I thought, man, that's awesome!"

Chapter 46

Hamlet: to Revenge or Not to Revenge

Our second workbook was *The Tragedy of Hamlet*, and Larry challenged the prisoners to consider alternatives to Hamlet's revenge of his father's murder. It is a difficult topic for prisoners to confront, so Larry introduced the play with his characteristically low-key style:

> *Tell me if this has ever happened to you: Your uncle kills your father and marries your mother as he steals your inheritance. Your good friends try to trick you into your grave, but you trick them into theirs instead. You accidentally kill your girlfriend's father, so she goes insane and kills herself. Her brother starts hunting to kill you, and you mother dies from poison that was intended for you. When it's all said and done, you kill your crazy girl's brother and he kills you—but not before you finally kill your uncle. It was a rough month, to say the least.*
>
> *Okay, even if you can't relate to Hamlet's specific circumstances, it is simple to relate to his condition. We have all felt the pain of loss, betrayal, perceived injustice, and the pressure of revenge. Hamlet is fighting the torment of what he could've done or should've done, or how he might have prevented the outcome. How many times have you laid there in bed fighting the torment of what you could've done, or should've done, or how you might*

have prevented the outcome? Do you know what separates you from Hamlet? Four hundred years. That's it. We all share his condition of feeling vulnerable, scared, conflicted, pressured. We also share his courage, integrity, pride, sense of honor, and deep desire for justice.

We are all heroes in our own tragedies.

Then he explores the "prison of expectation" that Hamlet is in, and the reason inmates feel the same pressure to revenge any perceived injustice:

The "Tragical History" of a prisoner's life seems to be one of many abuses, and therefore one with many justifications for revenge. Shakespeare has articulated an issue at the very heart of behavior in our society. You see, Hamlet is chasing honor for his family's name because that is what was expected of him. You are expected to seek vengeance for wrongs done to your family, even when you do not want to do it. In fact, to not seek vengeance is seen as cowardly and disgraceful to your family, and to a large extent your society.

We relate to Hamlet because he is in the same kind of "prison of expectation." His father has returned from the dead not to tell Hamlet how much he loved him, not to apologize for all the times that he worked late. He returned to make Hamlet revenge his death! It is that prison of expectation that we can relate to.

Hamlet *is not offering you hypocritical advice against revenge; it is reminding you that the choice really is yours to make! No matter what kind of social prison we are placed in, we are all empowered to make choices that are rooted in what we want, and not what others expect of us.*

Our workbooks were being used by nearly one hundred students: approximately twenty in the SHU program and thirty in my Correctional Education capstone course in general population, plus close to fifty in my Shakespeare class on campus. Every week, when I met with Larry to work on the next workbook, we also reviewed the homework of our students. I enjoyed reading some of the best—and worst—responses to our considerations and asking Larry to guess whether they were written by a campus student or a prisoner in SHU or population. It was often hard to tell. After considering our students' responses to his considerations, Larry spoke a response into my tape recorder, which I then typed up into a handout to the students that was distributed by the prison.

"That's really cool!" he said when he heard what one of the students had written about Hamlet's urge to revenge. "I like that the guy—"

"Or girl," I reminded him.

"That's true—or girl—is considering why Hamlet wants to kill his uncle: it's not for any noble reason; it's for selfish reasons."

"You're right," I told him. "It's a prisoner."

"Yes!" he shouted, smacking the table. "That's the idea behind real change. The idea is that we make them question things that we don't question. We don't question why we feel the urge to revenge, we don't question even what revenge is. We don't question any of these things. The idea is not to give them the answers, but to make themselves question."

Chapter 47

Othello: Girl Meets Boy

"I think this is my best work ever! I think I raised some really cool issues," Larry said as he handed me a stack of handwritten papers, this week's installment on our third workbook. "I can't wait to see what you think, man!"

As I looked over the pages, he fidgeted nervously. He bounced his leg, drummed his fingers on his Shakespeare book. Finally, he reached into his bag and unwrapped a Little Debbie cake. I never ate food in front of prisoners; it would seem rude because I couldn't legally share it with them. Larry usually did the same, but after ten years without access to Commissary (the prison's mini-mart), the luxury was getting the better of him and junk food became his passion. He spent a chunk of his weekly paycheck on Little Debbie cakes (the rest he sent home to Mom for his education fund).

"Look at me," he said between bites. "I've gained seventy pounds since I left the SHU!"

The Tragedy of Othello is the third of Shakespeare's "criminal tragedies," and it is an important one for prisoners to study. Racial issues are especially sensitive and susceptible to misunderstanding in prison. At one prison I had visited before starting my own program, I was told that prisoners have threatened to kill one another over conflicting interpretations of this play, and I believed it. Hundreds of years ahead of his time, in *Othello* Shakespeare presents a controversial look at biracial marriage—and murder. A black man marrying, and then killing, a white woman is dangerous stuff!

Once again, Larry created a workbook that invited prisoners to look deeply into the text, and into themselves, but he opened with a lighthearted introduction:

> *Girl meets boy. Usually, you would expect a nice love story to follow. But, as most of us know, love is not always so predictable—or always so nice. Of all the experiences we go through, love is sometimes the most pleasurable, and sometimes it is the most painful. It is also one of the most used story lines of storytellers, and* The Tragedy of Othello *is no exception. However, it is unlikely that you will ever read a story that captures the misery of love's parasite—jealousy—as well as it is captured in Shakespeare's play. Anyone who has experienced the tail side of love's coin will sympathize with Othello's misery. The image of the betraying act that attaches itself to the victim's thought like a leech that won't let go. The pain, the anger, the hatred, the confusion, the blame, the guilt, and oh the torment! Despite the universal experiences of love and jealousy, the actions and reactions spawned by the act of betrayal are as diverse as their justifications: some simply live a lie to avoid the misery; some sever the ties to the loved one; some even take the life of the perpetrator. For a seasoned warrior, therapy for betrayal is most often violent. Othello is again no exception.*

The considerations that follow each act of the play raise questions of morality, jealousy, envy, and the roles they play in criminal choices. Larry challenges prisoners to accept responsibility for their actions in a consideration titled "Your Mother":

At the end of the play, after Othello kills his wife, one of the characters raises a great question: "Is this the noble Moor whom our full senate call all in all sufficient?" So, is it? Or is it really Iago, the instigator behind the scenes? Who among us cannot identify our Iago somewhere in our lives? But the fact is, no one can make you be anything that is not already you, even if that you is buried deep inside, no? You may say, "If Iago had not done such and such, Othello would not have done such and such." If your mother was not forced to work away from home, she could have paid more attention to you and you might not have done such and such, but should your mother be in prison for what you have done? Who is responsible for what you do?

Accepting responsibility for one's actions is an essential first step toward rehabilitation. Larry did indeed raise some "cool issues."

Chapter 48

"Shakespeare Saved My Life"

Now that Larry was out of segregation and we were able to have normal conversations sitting side-by-side, without a steel door between us, I wanted to ask him to elaborate on what he had written in that survey he had handed me when he left the SHU.

"What did you mean," I asked him, "when you said that Shakespeare saved your life?"

"I meant it both ways: literally and figuratively," he told me. "Literally, Shakespeare saved my life. For so many years, I had been really self-destructive, on the razor's edge every day. I'm confident that I would've done something drastic and ended up on death row. Or I would've one day found the courage to take my own life. So literally, he saved my life."

It sounded like he was talking about suicide, but I couldn't believe it—I didn't want to believe it.

"And I meant it figuratively," he continued. "Shakespeare offered me the opportunity to develop new ways of thinking through these plays. I was trying to figure out what motivated Macbeth, why his wife was able to make him do a deed that he said he didn't want to do just by attacking his ego: 'What, are you soft? Ain't you man enough to do it?' As a consequence of that, I had to ask myself what was motivating me in my deeds, and I came face-to-face with the realization that I was fake, that I was motivated by this need to impress those around me, that none of my choices were truly my own.

"And as bad as that sounds, it was the most liberating thing I'd ever experienced because that meant that I had control of my life. I could be anybody I wanted to be. I didn't have to be some fake guy that my buddies wanted me to be. When I started reading Shakespeare, I was still in segregation; that circumstance didn't change. But I wasn't miserable anymore. Why? The only thing that was different was the way that I saw myself. So the way that I felt about myself had to be the source of all my misery. I'm of the opinion that we are the source of our misery; we perpetuate our own misery. And that realization is empowering! So Shakespeare saved my life, both literally and figuratively. He freed me, genuinely freed me."

From down the hall, we heard the officers turn on their radio to a country music station. Larry was startled. He looked around. It took him a few seconds to figure out where the sound was coming from. After ten years in isolation, he was unaccustomed to processing so many external stimuli. I tried to refocus his attention.

"Where do you think you would be now without Shakespeare?"

"I wouldn't be anywhere I am today, I know that," he replied. "I'd either be in deeper trouble—tried to escape and been in worse trouble than I was—or maybe I would've just that one day developed the courage to...you know what I mean?"

"Suicide?" I asked, hesitantly.

"Heck, yeah," he replied. "I was ready to go! I can't tell you how much I was."

I just looked at him. I had no idea.

"Hey," he said. "Don't get me all choked up. You're gonna make me all sad and teary-eyed, and I'm a big strong convict."

"Why?"

"I don't know why, man. 'Cause I'm really just glad to be where I am." He took a deep breath. "*Whew!*"

"It's a happy thing."

"Yeah. Very much so. But it's like, I don't know, you get back to where you were, and you're that close...I'm getting all sad. Not sad, but choked up."

"You're alive."

"I don't think being dead worried me too much. Obviously, it must have somewhat. I can honestly say the one reason that I didn't do it, and there may be other subconscious reasons, but the one reason is I kept picturing the impact on my loved ones. I was more worried about how they would take it. I didn't want to hurt them anymore."

"Good."

"Yeah. I mean, it was a good thought. But the point is, the being dead part never worried me. It seemed like a very plausible alternative. So that's not even what makes me the happiest. I like being alive, I like my life, but what makes me the happiest is that I just really feel like I can go anywhere and do anything. I make decisions now 'cause I want to. Just the liberty in it, the freedom in it, that's what makes me the happiest. So maybe that's why I got choked up."

I was speechless. I had worked with this prisoner for more than three years, but I had no idea that Shakespeare—and I—had that kind of impact on him. I had never had that kind of impact on anyone. I had never saved anyone's life before.

I found myself wondering what his life would have been like had he been introduced to Shakespeare—or to a caring teaching on any subject matter—earlier in his life. There might have been one less man in prison—and one more man alive.

"You keep staring at me like that, man," said Larry, "and I am gonna start freakin' crying or something."

Chapter 49

Shakespeare Saved My Life

It wasn't until I started writing this book that I realized that Larry's comment applied to me as well. In addition to challenging me to break out of my "fear of boats" prison, there was another episode of Shakespeare saving my life—less metaphorically and more literally, in this case. It went back to my first experience when I started working in prison, through the PACE Institute at Chicago's Cook County Jail, providing literacy assistance to inmates studying for their GED. My first experience could easily have been my last.

After becoming intrigued about working in prison through a discussion with my husband's friend, I learned of the opportunity to do volunteer literacy work at the jail through the community service department of the publishing company where I worked full-time as a proofreader while putting myself through college. Every Friday night after work, a minivan drove six of us volunteers across the city to the massive jail complex at Twenty-Sixth Street and California.

One night, I noticed that there were only three of us in the van, and the other two seemed unusually quiet. When we arrived at the jail and entered the building, we were told that the security level at the facility had been increased. The check-in procedure this evening would include a—gulp!—strip search. Conducted very discreetly by a same-sex officer behind a curtain, the search did not really bother me. But I did wonder at the reason for such heightened security.

"Is this normal?" I asked the matronly officer as she scrutinized each article of clothing that I handed to her. Because I was so new to the world of incarceration, I had no idea whether this was routine or extreme. She merely shrugged and turned her attention to my socks. Whatever it was, the officers didn't seem to know…or want to tell.

When we arrived in the education wing, the director informed us that there had been an escape attempt the previous week. Several prisoners had managed to grab the guns from a couple of officers (or maybe the officers had been bribed), and at gunpoint, they held a group of hostages while negotiating their demanded release. Their hostages were the teachers and other volunteers, some of whom were riding to the prison in the van with me. The incident had happened the previous Friday night.

Friday nights were my usual schedule at the prison, but it just so happened that I was not there that Friday. My husband had wanted me to see a student production of *Othello* at his university that night. I don't recall why; he wasn't involved in the production, and neither were any of his students. Neither he nor I were Shakespeare enthusiasts at the time. (In fact, I ended up a Shakespeare scholar through another odd series of happenstances, but that's a subject for another book.)

In any case, on that night, when I could've been one of those teachers on the prison floor with a gun to her head, Shakespeare saved my life.

Chapter 50

Shakespeare Could Save Your Life Too

I was once interviewed by a local news reporter who asked the common questions: Why are you doing this? Why do you care about these prisoners?

"I do care about them," I replied, "but, hey, I also care about you and me. Most of these guys will be on the street one day, and when they move in next door to you or enroll in one of my classes on campus, I want them to be less violent than they were when they came to prison." If Shakespeare saves the life of a violent criminal, through rehabilitation, then he saves the life of potential future victims. At least, that's the conviction that drove my work during my decade in supermax.

My research confirmed that the program indeed had such an effect: lessening the likelihood of violent incidents in a population with extensive histories of violence. I studied the conduct records of twenty of the most long-standing and active participants in the program and found that their combined conduct history accounted for more than six hundred violent or Class A offenses (the most severe category), including weapons charges and assaults, in their "B.S." (Before Shakespeare) years. During their time in the program, there were only two charges total, and none was violent or Class A. In fact, of the hundreds of prisoners who have been in the program—some for months, some for years—not one committed a violent offense.

I had the opportunity to test my hypothesis one day. As usual, I was sitting surrounded by convicted killers. I had been working with most of these particular prisoners for years by then, and the group included Larry as well, so I felt comfortable asking the ultimate question:

"*Can* Shakespeare save lives?"

"Ah, nah..." answered Gilmore, our newest member.

The rest of the group remained silent. Larry was waiting to see how I wanted to respond to this rejection of what had become the fundamental principle of our program.

"I'm still working on you, Mr. Gilmore," I said with a good-hearted chuckle, and the others joined in.

I appreciated his honesty, and I had to admit that he could well be right. But, if he was, then I also had to face the fact that I may have been wrong all along, may have been wasting my time, may have accomplished nothing more than creating, as the argument goes, "smarter criminals."

Then Leonard spoke up: "I'd like to give my perspective on that."

He commanded respect through his deep booming voice, his large physical frame, and his extensive criminal record that included homicide of an officer. That's as extreme as it gets. But he was also very thoughtful and insightful, and he addressed the question deliberately, weighing every word.

"I believe," he began, "that there are some people who, if a program has the ability to reach a person's soul to a degree and allow that person to seek healing and redemption, I believe that some—not all, but some—may be prevented from walking across that line of no return. 'Cause once you do it, you can't go back. You can't bring that person back."

Another prisoner added that "most murders aren't some

passionately planned thing; most are just stupid circumstantial behaviors."

"Right!" said another. "Reactive."

"I believe," Leonard continued, "as a convict having been allowed to interact with Shakespeare, that you and this program have allowed people to release anger, to release thoughts of revenge, various forms of frustrated thoughts or confusions. And when those things cloud judgment, that's when things happen. I know for me, it has been an alternative outlet. And when you talk about the issue of murder, I believe that if an individual had a small alternative, a moment to think, a person to lean on, in that split second, it probably never would've happened."

"There is a large portion of that population—the murder population—that only need a slight influence to do different," added another. "Not necessarily good versus bad, but they may see a new approach for whatever it is that they're after. So, yeah, absolutely."

"We've saved a life?" I asked.

"Saved my life," said Larry.

"Has Shakespeare saved a *victim's* life?" I asked.

"Yes. For sure, it's saved one other person."

That was the answer I was hoping for. And it was echoed by another prisoner, who added: "At least *two*."

(Photo credit: Indiana State University)

Chapter 51

Doing Life

Man, I'm set for life! That's the good news.
The bad news is, I'm doing life.

That comment was uttered by one prisoner acknowledging that all of the drug money he accumulated through his criminal career was useless now that he was in prison. But there's life and there's *life*: that was the next lesson I learned.

It was the summer of our third year, and I was preparing for a performance of a Shakespeare script (scenes from *Macbeth*, *Hamlet*, and *Othello*) written by the SHU prisoners. Because segregated prisoners could not come out of their cages to perform their scripts, I enlisted another group of prisoners from open population. Like the prisoners I worked with in segregation, this group consisted almost entirely of convicted killers, most of them serving what they called "all day": that is, life. But I learned that not all life sentences are the same. There's life—and there's life *without*.

For example, Patrick (who was playing Hamlet) had a life sentence, but he expected to be paroled in a few years. James (playing Othello) had a life sentence, was released once, violated his parole, and would be paroled again. (By the time this book is in print, he will be on the streets.) Larry, on the other hand, had life without the possibility of parole. He did not even have the right to file an appeal of his sentence, having waived that right nearly twenty years ago in his original sentence hearing when he was only seventeen years old.

Even those carrying sentences numbering hundreds of years were better off than Larry; at least they had a number to negotiate with. Joe (with his long hair in a ponytail, playing Lady Macbeth) managed to reduce his sentence by a hundred years. Dustin (our Macbeth) was sentenced to 199 years but reduced it to fifty. With time cuts and good behavior, he could be out before he reaches the age of fifty.

And then there is the discrepancy in the way in which the crime is interpreted. Just as there is life and *life*, there is murder and *murder*. Larry was under the influence of drugs, alcohol, and peer pressure. Jon (playing the villain Iago) killed two rival drug dealers in a calculated act of revenge; he could get out at the age of forty-two. Greg (our resident singer-songwriter with a melodious and gentle voice) premeditatedly killed both of his parents, shooting them as they slept; he'll be only thirty-five when he's released.

Like Greg and Dustin and Patrick, Larry was a teenager at the time of his conviction. On the other hand, other prisoners I worked with committed the same crime as adults. For example, Dan committed murder in his twenties and will serve thirty years. Leon was in his twenties and will serve thirty years. Jack was in his twenties when he premeditatedly killed his wife, and then he killed a man in prison. But after serving less than twenty years, he was released. No matter how much I learned in prison, there were some things I would never understand.

Larry is, in fact, the only prisoner I've ever met who was convicted as a juvenile and is serving life without parole. There is much legal debate currently on the unconstitutional nature of sentencing juveniles to life in prison. The argument is based on the idea that teenagers are most capable of rehabilitation. Through his good work in the Shakespeare program, in college, in other prison programs and job assignments, as well as in his acceptance of responsibility for his crime, Larry consistently demonstrated evidence of rehabilitation for nearly ten years. But every request for the right to appeal his sentence was denied.

No matter what he does, he will never leave prison.

Chapter 52
Romeo and Juliet

In the summer of 2006, after creating full-length workbooks of more than one hundred pages for each of the three criminal tragedies of Shakespeare—*Macbeth*, *Hamlet*, *Othello*—Larry had completed his "quarantine" time and joined the group in population. Immediately, he was recognized as the leader of the program, and we were ready to take on our greatest challenge yet: to create an adaptation of *Romeo and Juliet* geared toward at-risk teens. As always, Larry wrote the workbook that guided our work and was geared toward the intended audience. His introduction challenged our young readers: "Are you ready for the big leagues?"

> *When it comes to literature, Shakespeare is equivalent to 2-Pac in the rap industry, Led Zeppelin in the rock industry, Michael Jordan in the world of basketball, or Muhammad Ali in the world of boxing. He is the man! For the past four hundred years, he has had no rival! Maybe you associate Shakespeare to that "high falutin'" class of society, but that is not Shakespeare's fault, and you are mistaken if you think he targeted that class.*
>
> *Shakespeare is telling our story! He is telling the story of complex, conflicted people who are facing real issues, who have real problems, who know what it's like to lose, who know what*

it's like to cling to the edge, and who know what it feels like to be lost. But unlike many who attempt to use our circumstances to demean us, Shakespeare uncovers the power in these circumstances and offers you the tools to shape the life that you truly desire.

How can four-hundred-year-old stories do that? These stories are not merely "good stories"; they are tools that can give you back the power that the world, and you yourself, has deprived you of. When you think about the choices Macbeth makes, or the pressures Hamlet feels, you are confronted with fundamental principles that are important in our culture: honor, pride, conscience, ego. What do these words mean—to you? Make no mistake about it: this is not a simple thing to do. Shakespeare is not a cartoon or TV show used for simple entertainment. It is not a movie where your heroes and villains are obvious roles. These stories require you to actually think! I don't mean the kind of thought required just to follow what is happening in the story. I mean the kind of thought that requires you to figure out who the hero is, and who the villain is, or even what it means to be a hero in the first place.

You are going to have to dig inside yourself and come face-to-face with parts of you that you never knew existed. And, yes, the language is tough. These facts aren't meant to scare you away. I just thought that you should know that this is no cake walk. But I have every confidence that you are more than capable of stepping up into the "big leagues" of intellect. Others may want to water things down for you, because they see you as mere juveniles.

But I know that you are not simple-minded kids. Some of you have had experiences in life that sixty-year-old men will never have. Some of you have had enough hardships to last a lifetime. And some of you are smarter than the great majority of adult prisoners I have met in my thirteen years in prison. I was also just a juvenile when I became a prisoner, and I allowed these circumstances to define me as just that for many years. You can take back the power that you have been deprived of when you stop letting others define you as "kids," as "prisoners," as "outcasts," or whatever other labels people imprison you with. Only you can give them the power to do that, and only you can take that power from them. This prison that we're in physically doesn't matter. We were prisoners before we got here, and we'll be prisoners when we leave here unless we realize that we're fighting the wrong battle.

What matters is your own psychological prison—and you can break those chains. What have you got to lose? What else do you have to do? The worst that can happen is that you miss one television show. The best that can happen is that you find true freedom.

In addition to the workbook, we filmed a short video introducing our juvenile audience to the play of *Romeo and Juliet* and to six prisoners who—like Romeo—committed murder as teenagers: Patrick at eighteen, Jon at eighteen, Larry at seventeen, Steve at sixteen, James at sixteen, Dustin at fourteen. In the film, they speak directly to the teenage audience, telling them about the story of Romeo and Juliet and how it relates to them, trying to convince them to turn their lives around before it's too late—before they end up with life in prison.

I brought the video into some of the alternative high schools near my campus. This was a tough audience: I worried that we wouldn't be able to get them to turn their lives around, but there was one kid in particular, covered in tattoos and piercings, who I couldn't even get to turn his chair around and face the TV. Pointedly, he ignored the impassioned pleas of Patrick, of James, of Dustin.

And then Larry came on the screen.

"I don't know, man," Larry says in an unstaged, honest moment. "It just keeps going through my head that I didn't listen, you know, to these good-intentioned older guys telling me, 'Hey! If you don't straighten up your life, here's what's gonna happen.' I didn't listen, so I don't know what makes me think that you're listening now."

The tattooed kid turned around. He was actually looking at the screen!

"I mean, it's true," Larry continues, "all of it's true. But here's the thing, man. The big problem isn't trouble—well, obviously, it sucks—but the big problem is that twenty years from now, you're gonna look back and see that your life hasn't changed. You haven't gone anywhere, man. You're still just that same scared little kid you were at fourteen."

That got them all listening—and thinking. Here's what some of them wrote in response to the video (with all misspellings intact):

> *I'm 17 years old, I've been to juvy 2 times in my life for battery and theft/breaking in entering. I'm the one who said that Shakespere was retarted and there was no point to it. But hearing it from you guys and not a boring teaher is making it a lot better.*
>
> *I leon that the story is real well it like real life, that what I like about it. Even today world you got yo own craw and yo own side of town. I cant even remember how mane time I been at a pratty or something and people stared fighting over north side and south side stuff.*

And, amid the doodles of a disinterested teenager, here is what the tattooed kid wrote:

> *Well yea I was leasoning. Why? Becaes yall was talking about something. I mean yall was talking about how fucked up it can be if you make the worng chouies. If yall was talking about bullshit,*

prulbe woulda want to sleep. So I trying to say I leason to people than can help me.

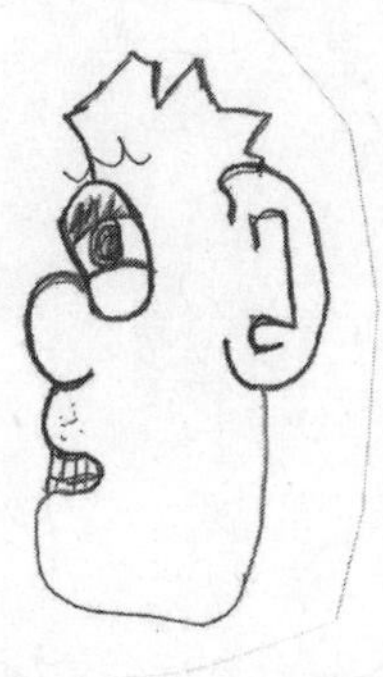

I understand what he is saying when he said you think the streets are your comfort but the streets love no one, and being in the streets just pull you in deeper into a bad life. That inspires me./

CHAPTER 53

Romeo and Juliet for Youth Incarcerated as Adults

At Wabash Valley Correctional Facility, the YIA unit houses the Youth Incarcerated as Adults: teenagers serving long sentences, often life, in an adult prison. The former SHU manager, Ken Gilchrist, was now the manager of this unit, and I offered to include some of these kids in our *Romeo and Juliet* project with the assumption that he would immediately recognize what a positive role model Larry and the others could be. After all, Larry had been a youth incarcerated as an adult himself. But whereas Larry, at age seventeen, was thrown in among hard-core adult prisoners to start his life term, I learned that the Department of Corrections now had an absolute rule prohibiting any interaction whatsoever between juvenile and adult offenders. "They can't come in here," Gilchrist informed me. "You'll have to make a video for them." So that's what we did, expanding on the video I had brought into the alternative high schools.

The Shakespeare group in open population spent the next year writing an original adaptation of the play geared toward what they affectionately called these "badass kids." They didn't focus on the love story, though. Instead, they focused on the peer pressure that can push a good kid like Romeo into murder, and they interwove their own stories of how they each became a teenage killer and what their prison experience had been like. Sort of a *Scared Straight* through Shakespeare. They called their adaptation *Tybalt Must Die!* This was very much a group effort, and although Larry was recognized and respected as the leader, he chose to play the lesser role of Benvolio. It is a small part, often overlooked in productions of the play, but Larry saw Ben as "the voice of reason" who tries to talk the others into a peaceful resolution to their conflicts. At the end of each scene, Larry stepped forward and spoke into the camera. The action onstage froze and the lights dimmed as he addressed the teenage audience with probing questions such as, "Why do these people feel such 'blind hatred' for one another? Who do you hate blindly?" and "Why does Romeo give in to his buddies? Why do *you*?"

The approach he was taking with the incarcerated juveniles was the same one that had worked so successfully with the adult prisoners. "They're no different," Larry said. "They just have a shorter attention span." One day, when I made a reference to these "hard-core kids," he taught me another important lesson.

"You cannot use those words! What we do not want to do is isolate these kids as 'hard-core.' That will only encourage the celebrity they find in the results of their behaviors. You have to think of these kids in need of your help as just that: kids in need of your help! Even you, great doc, are not above the influence of subconscious prejudice. Wow! Was that a tongue-lashing, or what? No, man, I'm just kidding."

But that was what he always said when he was not kidding.

"So what should we say?" I asked him. "What would have spoken to you as a 'kid in need'?"

"It doesn't really work that way. It's not what someone says to a kid that really matters; it is more the experience. Trust me, they have heard it all. People throughout history have searched for the 'magic words,' as you already know. These videos may have a powerful moment when they see us kids doing life in prison. For that time, it is a really strong deal, but it does not deal with the cancer…it is just a powerful moment. Their self-image, insecurities, social icons—all that is not impacted, and *that* is the cancer! Hopefully, we can create an experience that makes them indict these cancers, and that will not happen but through sidestepping all their little defense mechanisms. Basically, sneak attacks that anticipate their defenses and then smash their reasoning! It is not quite as cruel as Socrates, but it is that same method. Man! I just realized that!"

Chapter 54
Balance

Prison is a stressful environment: for those who live there, work there, and even those who voluntarily enter.

"I'm glad we live an hour away," my husband once said to me, "or I'd make you drive around the block for an hour before I let you come in." True, that hour on the open country highway, with rap music blasting, helped begin the process of unwinding. But it took a good bit more than an hour to come down from the day's new discoveries and insights, worries and plans for the week ahead. A glass or two (or three or four) of cheap red wine sipped while I related the day's events to Allan became a weekly ritual.

But it wasn't a healthy way to detox over the years, especially when I started developing heart issues, inheriting my parents' chronic high blood pressure. The stress was compounded by concerns about my aging parents' declining health and about their financial needs, which I worried about not being able to meet if I did not obtain that all-important tenured position at the university. I had to find a healthy way to destress.

I took up yoga. Even if I was the oldest kid in the class, and even if I couldn't touch my toes, I enjoyed the physical and emotional balance that it offered. The drama of my Friday nights was followed by yogic calm on Saturday morning: *Ommmm.* It was the perfect antidote for prison stress. If I wasn't teaching Shakespeare in prison, I would have loved to teach yoga (if I were qualified to do so). The yoga classes that I was taking always ended with a progressive relaxation exercise done while lying on the floor in the pose that's called "corpse." Thinking it would be a good warm-up to begin our rehearsal session at the prison one day, I introduced a modified version of the technique.

"Stand up, everyone," I said. Fifteen prisoners got up from their chairs.

"Spread out a little bit." They did, wondering what I was going to ask next.

"Now, close your eyes."

What?!

"Uh…Dr. Bates, I don't think—"

"Don't worry," I assured them. "I won't ask you to do anything…weird."

They looked skeptical.

"Trust me."

Trust: that's the key word in prison, and it's not earned easily. And you never, ever ask anyone in prison to close his eyes. The fact that every one of them did was the strongest evidence I've ever had of how much they did, in fact, trust me.

But I was a failure as a yoga teacher; most of them concluded that it was weird. Nevertheless, I continued to enjoy my weekly sessions with the group at the local Y. Teetering on one leg with hands folded in prayer position made me more balanced, mentally and physically. Eventually, I even touched my toes.

Chapter 55

Tybalt Must Die!

In the summer of 2007, when the *Romeo and Juliet* adaptation script was finished and ready for filming, the group performed in the prison chapel before an audience of invited guests that included all of the top administration of the prison, the media, and, most importantly, their own family members.

After years without contact, Larry had reunited with his own family—mother, two brothers, countless nieces and nephews—thanks to Shakespeare. He now had something positive to talk about in letters and phone calls. He wrote to his brothers about his work in the Shakespeare program, and he encouraged his nieces and nephews to stay in school. He invited them to come to the Shakespeare performance, excited to be receiving visits after so many years. (The only visitors most segregated prisoners receive are their attorneys, with whom they converse by telephone and through a glass partition. Family visits are even more restrictive: the prisoner sits in a closed-circuit video booth while his relative sits in another booth in a different part of the prison. Few prisoners have family members devoted enough to drive for hours to talk to their loved one through video.)

I got to meet Mom and both of Larry's brothers when they attended the Shakespeare performance. No doubt their presence made him especially nervous when I asked him to give the introductory address. He spent weeks preparing his speech, entire days struggling with just the opening words: "Welcome, everyone!" He read from his handwritten script in our rehearsal session, then crossed it off, saying, "Man, that sounds retarded!"

Now, with the cameras rolling and the audience watching, he held his script tightly in his shaking hands...and never even looked at it.

"Shakespeare," he began, "saved my life. I know that sounds crazy, but it's true. I swear!" And he raised his right hand as if swearing an oath.

"The Shakespeare program began in the segregation unit," he continued, "and I'd spent ten and a half years in those units. I went in as a nineteen-year-old kid, and I didn't get out till I was a thirty-year-old man. While most people spend their twenties trying to find their place in this world, I spent every single day of my twenties pacing my cell in isolation, trying to find reasons not to leave this world. And that's when I was introduced to Shakespeare through Dr. Bates. I was at the crossroads in my life. I wasn't sure if I would find the courage to stay where I was or to go beyond where I was. To...to kill myself."

From somewhere in the audience, I could hear a gasp. I wondered if it was Larry's mom. I wondered if she knew that he had been to that point in his life. He had told me that he had written a suicide letter—but did he send it?

"It was the right moment for me, so I said yes, I wanted to study Shakespeare. She left me a speech by King Richard the Second, which he was expressing from his own supermax dungeon four hundred years before. I just couldn't believe that this guy was pacing around in his own dungeon, just like me. That was my first exposure to Shakespeare, and it would literally change the rest of my life."

Standing off to the side, trying to be inconspicuous, I became aware of one of the photographers turning his camera toward me, and I wondered why.

"So the last few years that I was in segregation I spent analyzing and discussing Shakespeare through a hole in a steel door with a group of other prisoners. We'd discuss what we read, and everything would come up for discussion. We'd try to define these terms like *honor*, *integrity*, etc. It really forced me to find some kind of substance to these terms that shape our lives. I was forced to look into a mirror, basically, at myself, to give these things real meaning. That changed the way I felt about everything, about others, about myself. I was literally digging into the very root of myself while digging into Shakespeare's characters. For instance, I couldn't say that Hamlet's impulse for revenge was honorable if I couldn't tell you what honor is, and I couldn't. I still can't tell you what honor is, but I can tell you some of the things that it's not, and Hamlet's revenge is one of them.

"I eventually left segregation and Dr. Bates continued to allow me to work with the program. She asked if I could re-create my thinking patterns, how my two selves came into conflict with one another. So I basically re-created my own experience, and put it on paper so she could gather them together and bring it back there where these guys are going through what I was going through: literally just fighting for their lives. I wanted to challenge them to go through what I went through, to try to define these terms because these things drive our lives and we don't even know what they are. I think it's critical to get these people to start addressing these questions.

"And now we want Shakespeare to work for other people as it's worked for us, as a tool for use, not just a compilation of great stories. We want to bring it to these juveniles, who are right now still shaping the rest of their lives, and hopefully we can counter the same hollow principles that we built our lives on. That's our goal, and that's what we're doing. Thank you."

Before he could leave the stage, the audience jumped to their feet in a standing ovation. Larry stood there awkwardly, but he was beaming. I looked over at Mom. I thought I saw her wipe away a tear. I was beaming like a proud mother myself. And that is what the photographer captured.

The prisoners' adaptation did not cover the entire play; it didn't even include Juliet. It focused on Romeo and his peers, and it ended with act 3 when Romeo kills his rival Tybalt. Sirens blared and an officer came onstage to arrest Romeo for manslaughter. One by one, each of the actors stepped forward and spoke, starting with Romeo: "Shakespeare wrote this play four hundred years ago, but it still applies to teenagers today. I came to prison at age eighteen for murder, and I'm serving a life sentence."

The actor playing the officer spoke next: "I came to prison at age sixteen for murder, and I'm serving a life sentence."

The murdered Tybalt got up from the floor, dusted himself off, and said, "I came to prison at eighteen for a double murder, and I'm serving two fifty-five-year sentences."

Father Montague (Romeo's dad) stepped forward: "I came to prison as a sixteen-year-old, with two murder convictions, and I'm serving two eighty-year sentences."

Romeo's pal Mercutio came back onstage: "I came to prison at the age of fourteen, for murder, and I'm serving a sentence of 199 years."

The last one to speak up was Benvolio, the voice of reason, played by Larry: "I came to prison at the age of seventeen for murder with a sentence of life without the possibility of parole. I will never go home."

In unison, the group spoke the closing lines: "We hope you learn from Romeo's mistake—and from our own."

Lights out. Another standing ovation.

Chapter 56

Killer in the Classroom

The *Romeo and Juliet* project impacted my on-campus teaching in an unexpected way. At the time, I was leading a schizophrenic academic life: teaching Shakespeare in prison while teaching children's literature courses for future elementary school teachers on campus. Kids and killers. I never thought the twain would meet, but once again, I learned an important lesson from my prisoners.

Naïvely, I had assumed that "at-risk" youth needed an intervention during their teenage years, and that's why I brought our *Romeo and Juliet* video into the alternative high schools. But as I listened to the prisoners sharing their life stories, it became apparent that each of these men who had committed murder as a teen had started down that road at a much younger age. I asked each of them the question I had earlier asked Larry: "At what age did your criminal career begin?" Their responses took me by surprise.

Dustin: "Twelve. Started off with runaways, criminal mischief."

Steve: "Ten. Playing hooky from school, selling dope."

Larry: "Ten. Stealing from Kmart."

Jon: "Eight. Keying cars, vandalism."

James "Eight. Stealing pop from the store whenever I was thirsty from playing ball."

Patrick: "Seven—"

Me: "Seven?"

Patrick: "Seven. Calling in false fires, out past curfew, drinking under age."

Me: "*Seven?!*"

Kevin, the only prisoner in the group who was not serving a murder sentence, summed it up by saying, "What a child experiences between the ages of seven and ten will determine his actions as a teenager and an adult."

I thought this was crucial information for future elementary school teachers, and I found that it was not addressed in their education courses. "Killer in the Classroom" was the title of a presentation that I prepared for the future elementary school teachers. The title got their attention, and the prisoners' stories kept them riveted for the full hour.

While none of these prisoners placed blame on their teachers for turning them into criminals, all of them had advice for how a teacher could spot a troubled child in her classroom and how to reach out to him. They also pointed out some of the ways in which even well-intentioned actions could backfire. Jon related his experiences as a boy who, because his father's job required frequent transfers, was often the new kid in school. He admitted to engaging in some juvenile mischief, but nothing requiring the harsh treatment he received. One teacher, having heard of his reputation as a troublemaker, singled him out at the start of the school year—literally, singled him out. She made him spend the semester behind a partition in the back of the room, separated from the rest of the students. Over time, that led to his rejection of the teacher, of his schoolwork, of school. That led to the streets, to drugs, to violence. Jon connected the dots by concluding, "Stick me behind a partition, and I grow up and kill someone."

My end-of-semester surveys always showed this presentation

to be the most impactful moment of the semester. It was a lesson that I knew my students would remember when they started working with little Larrys, Dustins, and Patricks. And I believed that it, too, could save lives.

Chapter 57

Hands that Kill Can Also...Sew?

In addition to the Shakespeare program, Wabash Valley Correctional Facility had another unusual program that provided a creative outlet for its prisoners in general population: quilting. It was remarkably popular among many prisoners and, like Shakespeare, demonstrated that activities that might seem effeminate can be embraced by the most macho of men. Furthermore, the quilts made by the prisoners were donated to charitable causes, such as battered women and families of deceased veterans. The quilts were accomplished works of art in their own right and were displayed at the Indiana state fair, on the news, and in the offices of the top administrators of the facility.

When I learned that some members of the Shakespeare program in general population were also quilters, I was amazed that they found the time to engage in two such demanding hobbies in addition to a schedule that often included a full-time job and college classes every night. They told me that they recited Shakespearean texts while sewing, entertaining their quilting comrades while memorizing their lines.

One Shakespearean quilter, Dustin, had been a member of the drama group in open population since our first production in 2004. When he joined, he was the youngest, and shyest, member of the group, and he limited his role to simply reading a few sentences of introduction to the scenes and speeches that the others performed. But the following year, he agreed to take on the lead role of Macbeth, and his acting ability really became apparent. That, coupled with his handsome Brad Pitt looks, caused one of our audience members to ask if he was an actor by profession. Alas, he never was, and never will be.

Entering an adult prison while still a juvenile, he, like Larry, was a small, scared kid in a tough adult world. He responded with violence. His was one of the most extensive conduct histories among those I examined: nearly one hundred offenses in his pre-Shakespearean years.

"He just wanted to hurt you," an officer once told me. "And if he couldn't do it physically, then he would do it emotionally."

"I'll do whatever you want me to" is the refrain I always heard from Dustin, and it was uttered in a sincere, not sarcastic, tone of voice. Over the years, he proved to be one of the most productive and essential members of our group. True to his word, he always did whatever I asked of him, stepping into whatever role was vacant or writing whatever additional text was needed.

Even the officer quoted above eventually had to admit—as Sgt. Harper said of Larry: "If Shakespeare made him change, I'm impressed."

Dustin's contributions to our *Romeo and Juliet* project were especially valuable, with him not only playing the important role of Romeo's best friend Mercutio, but also sharing his insights as a troubled kid and the parallels between the Shakespearean character he portrayed on stage and his own character:

> *Mercutio is very hot-headed. He is big on how people's perceptions of him are. I was the same way. But my crimes are nothing like what Mercutio did out of loyalty to Romeo. There was no honor or*

justness in what I did. I was a self-absorbed, self-centered fourteen-year-old who cared little for anything or anyone else but myself.

His open and honest self-revelation spoke to the at-risk teens to whom I presented the video. They saw themselves in what he was saying, and they saw that they could easily end up like him. He never intended to kill anyone; it was the unexpected result of common teenage mischief. Even his effective stage presence was valuable, making our video powerful and riveting. Teenage girls stayed after class just to get another glimpse of him.

At the end of the public performance of our *Romeo and Juliet* adaptation at the prison, after the standing ovation and after the extended applause finally died down, Dustin came back on stage carrying a large parcel. Surprises are not usually a good thing in prison, but this one was.

"We want to thank Dr. Bates for all she's done for us," he began. And then he opened up the bag. "With a quilt."

Denim and black (my "prison colors"), it measured six feet by six feet and was made single-handedly by Dustin.

Wow! I was speechless as he handed it to me, and despite my conviction to never become emotional in prison, I was moved almost to tears. The guys could tell. I overheard one of them say, "Yeah, I thought we might get some squirts."

I hate to sew, can't even thread a needle. I couldn't imagine the time involved in cutting out 288 little squares of black cloth, white cloth, and different shades of denim and then painstakingly sewing them together. And then, on the reverse side, he had made an intricate design out of paisley-patterned cloths on a background of pale denim. The time, the talent, the thoughtfulness! It was hard to hold back the "squirts."

The quilt.

Chapter 58

Fears and Phobias

One day, I brought a video to watch with Larry: a Discovery Channel show that includes a reenactment of his hostage attempt in the SHU in 2000. I wondered if he had ever seen it.

"Oh here, let me help you," he said, jumping up from his chair to help the middle-aged officer who was struggling to wheel an unwieldy TV/VCR cabinet into our little classroom. Again, I couldn't help being impressed with his respectful demeanor with the officers. With the cabinet in place and plugged in, the officer inserted my tape into the little slot in the standard-issue TV/VCR combo while I sat down next to Larry. (I wished we could share a bag of popcorn.)

"As you watch your reenactment," I said to him, "let me know if there's anything that's not accurate."

The video opened with the announcer's dramatic voiceover: "Three letters strike fear into the hearts of prisoners: S-H-U...." The visuals showed the familiar ranges on the SHU where Larry lived for so many years.

"That's my cell," he said, pointing at the screen.

Momentarily, a prison official dressed in a business suit came on camera and stated gravely, "All of the prisoners in the Secured Housing Unit are dangerous...."

"That's not true," Larry said quietly, more to himself than to me.

"What?"

"They're not all dangerous."

The tape showed the official re-creating the movements of the officers during the hostage attempt, backing out of the range, crossing his hands to protect his face, as he described how these prisoners "with blood lust on their mind" came at them, "cutting and slashing." Then a photo showed the stab wound in Harper's shoulder. It was all very dramatic, very scary. Again, I found these behaviors difficult to reconcile with the man sitting next to me. I wanted to believe that he was a different person. That he was changed, permanently changed.

After the clip ended, I asked him, "Did that put you back into that mind-set, the 'blood lust'?"

"No," he replied. "I can't feel it. I mean, I remember it, but I just can't *feel* it anymore."

I asked Larry what his goal was in the hostage attempt.

"We had a list of demands," he told me. "We were gonna leave the cell 6 food slot open so we could have direct contact for medical, 'cause when guys needed medical they would be banging and screaming for hours, and them COs would just do nothing, man, nothing!"

"That was one of your demands?"

"Yeah."

"You risked your life to improve the conditions of your fellow prisoners? That's sweet."

"No no no, that's not sweet! It's ridiculous. For one, it's not gonna happen."

"But it wasn't, 'Let me out'?"

"No, there was no demand like that: 'Ship us out!' No."

"What was the reaction of the other prisoners on the range?"

"Silence."

"Really? I assumed cheering."

"Yeah, 'cause they're 'evil prisoners,'" he said with a chuckle.

"That's not true?"

"It's not true. We just happen to be in prison. We're still human, we have the same reactions: it's shocking. Places are silent when things go down. It's a shocking experience for everybody. You're just sitting there watching TV, all of a sudden this goes down, you're not getting rowdy, you're shocked by it. My instinct is always to get away from a fight."

"You know that it was Sgt. Harper who got you out for our session that first day?"

"Really? Well, I can say this about Mr. Harper: I didn't go out there to butcher this guy, and he knows that. I think that's why we don't have a problem to this day. I'm not saying we're buddies or anything, but I think he knows that if I was out there to kill him or hurt him real bad, I could've. I had him held by himself, pinned up against the wall, a knife in my hand. I could've been stabbing him the whole time, but I wasn't."

A thought occurred to me, and Larry picked up on my silence.

"What?" he asked.

"We're sitting here alone every week, unsupervised. Ever consider taking me hostage?"

"No. Never. Uninhibited truth here."

"Good."

"What could I get anyways?" he asked, pointing to my water bottle. "A vitaminwater?" He laughed and called out: "I need a vitaminwater and some French fries. Now!"

"That's rather insulting, isn't it?"

"Take you hostage. Man, what the—?!"

He laughed again, and I got up from our table. As I took the tape out of the VCR, I asked a question that I assumed one should never ask of a prisoner.

"Were you scared? When the extraction team came in?"

"No."

"Why not?"

"Well, I mean, you know there's a banging coming, so you just sort of get ready for that, psych yourself up for that. Maybe there isn't time to be afraid."

He seemed fearless, and he was teaching me to be more fearless myself, not only in my prison work, but also in helping me to recognize that unfounded phobias, like fear of flying or fear of sailing, were good examples of the types of "prisons" that we all put ourselves into.

"Is there *anything* that you're afraid of?" I asked.

"Yes!" he shouted, smacking the table with his hand for emphasis—a common gesture. "*Spiders!*" he said with a shudder. "Always have been."

"Come on, man," I wanted to say, "that's retarded." It was one thing for me, as a timid little girl, to have been afraid of insects growing up—but for a big tough convict?

"Are you kidding?" I said. "You have lived in dangerous environments all your life, in ghettos and in prisons, and your greatest fear is a tiny little harmless insect?"

"Ask my mom. She'd tell you: I would jump out of a *moving* car to get away from a spider." He slapped the table again. "No joke!"

Another lesson learned: even the toughest of criminals has his weakness. "We just happen to be in prison. We're still human."

Chapter 59

Sociopath or...

"Who Am I?"
To date, I have uncovered that I am:
Insecure, confident.
Stupid, intelligent.
Lame, funny.
Pessimistic, optimistic.
Deceitful, truthful.
A loyal friend, a loyal enemy.
A loving son, a hateful subject.
A killer, a lifesaver.
A captive, and a free man.

Larry read to me the self-reflective poem that he had written in his English 101 class (one of five college classes he was taking each semester). Then he asked me, "Do you think I'm a good man or a bad man?"

"How do you see yourself?"

"I think I'm a good guy, really. For two reasons. For one, I have a genuine compassion."

"Where do you see that?"

"I don't know. We'll get to that. And two, because I genuinely want to be better."

"What does 'better' look like to you?"

"What 'better' looks like to me is internal. I still have a great deal of cowardice in me in the sense that I still conduct myself in certain ways in certain settings; I'm still somewhat dictated by the environment as opposed to my genuine will in life. So being more courageous, detaching some of these strings in my life, having even greater insight into myself and even into human behavior—all this is my idea of 'better.'"

"Nothing to do with your sentence?"

"No, my sentence doesn't dictate that. I'm the happiest I've ever been in my life, and nothing's changed with my sentence. I am hopeful, though. I am working on an appeal, for the first time. It's so neat to reflect on myself of only five or six years ago and see the contrast. My life was so miserable! I convinced myself that I was powerless and 'myself' proved myself right. In almost fifteen years of prison, I had never fought to go home! My only aspirations were the idea of leaving one prison to go to another. How crazy is that?"

"So where do you see compassion in yourself?"

"Even as a kid, I hated them bullies that picked on people, or people that abused animals, and I ask myself, how can I be more sympathetic for a dog than for this guy that got his head busted open? I've never been without compassion, though some of my behaviors have seemed compassionless. But here's the thing: I still think compassion was the dominant part of my characteristic, strangely. You probably block it out. There are people I still don't have compassion for, but there are a lot more people at this stage in my life that I do have compassion for that I didn't before."

"One reporter accused you of being a sociopath, remember? 'His expansive enthusiasm camouflages a persistent sociopathy.'"

"I don't understand why my enthusiasm would camouflage that."

"Do you think you're a sociopath?"

"That sounds so scary. A sociopath is what?"

"Someone who kills on a whim."

"I don't think I've ever killed anybody on a 'whim.' It's hard for me to fathom that, having no emotions. I can't see doing something with no emotion. I can see doing it and not being tormented by what happens. But why do you do it? There has to be some emotional attachment. There has to be something that draws you to that act. I can see not being tormented; I can see that's a defense mechanism. If I feel I'm gonna be hurt, I have a defense mechanism. I just go numb. I don't let it attach itself to me, right?"

"You turn it off."

"Turn it off, right."

"Have you always had this kind of callousness?"

"No. I don't know when it developed, but it was definitely in my seg experience because I remember being absolutely distraught—how could I get in those states of suicide other than this great torment? I want to escape this by any means! I got to get out of this! So this callous developed through that experience. I mean, you're at the extremes. Either you develop this kind of callous, or you're gonna do something really regrettable. But you're not gonna settle in, nobody's gonna carry that kind of load."

"Do you think you'll have that for the rest of your life?"

"Yeah I do, I think it's a part of me. It's not one of those things that I have control over; it just happens. You just instinctively go there: This is where I need to be psychologically. This is where I'm safe. They're not gonna touch me, nobody."

"Nobody except yourself."

"Right. That is the bottom line. It is you."

"If you have this callous, what keeps you from killing people?"

"You don't get the callous before the deed, but after. It's a coping mechanism, not a proactive thing."

"But you're talking about this coping mechanism with a lot of confidence, so knowing that you can count on it to protect you from torment...."

"Right, so you're saying preemptively, I can do this and know that I can cope. But I don't know how to explain that it's not a weapon. Let me think it through. All this is thinking as I go. Hey, most of my thinking is on a 'whim,'" he said with a chuckle.

"You see where I'm going with this."

"Let's go."

"If you can handle anything—you know that nothing's going to torment you psychologically and you've survived the most extreme form of punishment—what stops you?"

"It's a great question, but the crazy thing is, it already presupposes—I don't know what 'presupposes' means, but I assume it means that it's already concluded—that that's what the person wants to do."

"Why don't you want to?" I kept urging because I knew that this was an important discovery that he needed to make, and he was almost there.

"Okay," he said at last. "For me, all my violence, all of it, related to the impression I was trying to make. I don't think I'll ever lose that desire to make impressions, but two things have changed. I've found different ways to make impressions: with my intellect or whatever. And I have more confidence in myself to not have the same insecurities to need to make those impressions. So even if I have this callous, I don't have the *incentive*. That's what's lacking."

"That's the key, right there."

"Yes, it is."

Chapter 60

Socrates

After spending four years discussing and examining Larry's past, we turned to speculating on his future.

"I don't have an idea of what my life will be like twenty years from now," he stated. "But I do want to excel in academics. I want to get the PhD, I really do. The idea excites me. And I'm excited 'cause, man, I really think we're getting there with our program, we're really reaching them. That excites me, to think where the program could go."

"You're a good teacher."

"I will be," he said with a proud smile.

I liked the confidence with which he made the assertion, though his request for permission to file an appeal of his sentence—permission just to *file*—had been denied.

"How did you get from contemplating suicide to saving lives?"

"That's difficult to say. For one, it's uncharted territory. I think most people that look at things like this, these psychologists, are from the outside looking in. For two, there's no one single thing, it's a cocktail of things. The whole being here at this end and now here at this end, it could be that when people fall the farthest down, they bounce back the highest. What's the opposite of 'tragedy'? Aristotle says that tragedy is the downfall of the protagonist through his own internal tragic flaw. Then what's the term for the story of a protagonist heading in the other direction? That is my story! Macbeth met me at his end and pointed me in the direction he vacated. In a strange twist of roles, this villain has served a very noble purpose."

"You said this was the best time of your life. Is that true?"

"Absolutely, this has been at least a couple of years that I've known this is the best time of my life. And it's not just a maintained thing—it keeps getting better. I'm stronger in those abilities, more able to influence my mood and shape the guy I want to be. The world just opens up, you really can do anything—okay, you can't fly—but you can shape your life. There really is nothing I can conceive of that I can't do. So without question, yes, absolutely the best time of my life, the greatest thing that ever happened to me. Forty years from now, I'm gonna owe the great things in my life to these times. This Shakespeare experience really is the key defining pivotal moment in my life."

He was beaming as he opened his book to start our work for the day. I was still trying to imagine where his life would go, whether he would get out one day, whether he would even get the chance to pursue his dream, but I didn't want to shatter the optimistic mood.

"After you get your PhD," I told him, "don't forget to come back to prison."

"Oh, yeah. It's been a big part of my life; it'd be hard to ignore it. Plus I don't think I'd have better insight anywhere else."

"You know what Socrates said about that."

"About what?"

"Going back after you gain your enlightenment: The Allegory of the Cave."

"That wasn't Socrates, was it? That was Plato, wasn't it?"

I was impressed. And he was right. It's from *The Republic*, in which Plato quotes Socrates.

"I did read that little cave thing, yeah!" he continued. "That was a cool story, man! These people come out and they had just seen shadows and had characterized all these shadows. That was their reality 'cause that was all that they knew. And then to come and find out they were just shadows of other real things. But! The challenge was in going back and trying to tell these people, 'Look, these shadows ain't real.' How can you tell somebody? 'I know it's real! You're a freakin' moron!'"

He had just presented, in his typical down-to earth style, a perfect summary of Plato's philosophical essay. And he was still on a roll.

"You know what?" he continued. "Them guys on the SHU might be seeing the real life, and everybody else is like, 'Man, they're crazy!' I thought about that before too: What if they're right? What if they got it all figured out, and I'm the one that's lost in this whole thing? You know, they all had these crazy conspiracies: 'They're putting things in the food! They got things in the chase ways, you gotta cover your vent!' or whatever their little paranoid scenarios were. And you're like, 'Hey, come on, you're crazy!' But then you're like, 'What if they're right? What if I'm the crazy one?' I think I see reality a certain way, but what if I'm the one that's warped? And that's what makes it easier for me to be maybe not sympathetic but to understand that, you know, this isn't just something they're doing. It's the condition. This is the way they see the world. It's not like they're trying to be this person. I know what I know based on whatever my experience is, and they know what they know because of their ordeal, right?"

"So now that you've gotten out of the cave and seen the shadows to be shadows—"

"How do you convince them? You just have to remember what it's like to know that that's a shadow. You know what I mean? You can't ever forget."

Chapter 61

Doing Good for Bad Done

Not only was Larry a good teacher, often making adept use of the Socratic method, but he also cared passionately about education. Soon after he enrolled in his first college courses, he became aware of the controversy over the topic of correctional education: Why should tax dollars support free education for criminals when law-abiding citizens have to go into debt to cover their college costs? It is a complex debate, and Larry contributed a well-argued essay that I published in *Indiana English*, a journal for which I serve as editor. He titled it "Doing Good for Bad Done." Here it is in abbreviated form:

> *There appear to be two arguments under one subject. The first is that offering educational programs for criminals is, in effect, creating smarter criminals. It is a very tough argument to debate. What makes this argument so tough to oppose is exactly what will undo the argument. The second argument is essentially a question: Why should we do good things for those who have done bad things?*
>
> *So, to the first argument: The developing mind of a criminal is just that—the developing of a criminal mind. But where do we find data to support that argument? It is not as though the assumed criminal lifestyle is charted and monitored. We are left*

to our assumptions; why would we assume otherwise? To assume that a criminal's developing mind is a developing criminal mind, we must assume that the very nature of every criminal is crime and that the only possible change in a criminal's behavior can be new criminal behavior.

Logic says that the only possible way to assume such a conclusion about a person is to already harbor a universal conclusion about the idea of such a person. "A tiger cannot change its stripes." Who among us has not deceived someone, kept something that did not belong to us, snuck out at night, "borrowed" Mom's car, or engaged in any number of such common youthful adventures? If we are arguing that such behavior can only develop, then what are we saying about ourselves? We have concluded that crime is not a nature, it is a choice, and any choice is influenced by our experiences and our circumstances. The only thing that really separates the criminal from us is the different experiences and circumstances. Why do we assume that educating a criminal is merely helping him commit more sophisticated crimes? Why can't we assume that an education can give this person the tools to make more acceptable choices?

Our second argument is "Why should we do good for bad people?" The answer is because "anything else would be bad." If we are not doing good for bad people, then we are doing bad for bad people. We should not be working on ways to do bad for isolated populations of people; rather, we should work on developing good no matter who is on the receiving end. That is our obligation to society.

The statistical evidence speaks for itself in favor of education for prisoners, but let me share with you my own experience. I have made terrible mistakes in my life, and one terrible thirty-second mistake thirteen years ago cost me my liberty. I was seventeen years old then, and I am now thirty. The furthest I made it in school was a week's worth of my freshman year of

> *high school. In fact, I have been locked away from society since a very early age. As a person of the world, I was pushed over by a good wind. My behavior was driven by what others expected of me and what was left for me as an example. Obviously, the world you are exposed to is critical to how you end up. The good news is that since that is true, such a person is really susceptible to positive influence by the change of the world around him. It is a very inspiring story, because I am indeed the living fossil of positive change, and that education is indeed a powerful tool for positive change. You see, I was living in a supermax segregation unit when I was exposed to an educational opportunity that reshaped the rest of my life. Education gave me not only a new confidence in making decisions for myself, but it also gave me more understanding and many more options. It helped develop my critical thinking skills, and made it possible to better weigh behaviors and consequences. It gave me new direction in life and in a real sense it saved my life.*
>
> *We cannot risk not helping. The vast majority of prisoners are going to return home. They are going to be our neighbors and they are going to be around our loved ones. The question really comes down to: what kind of prisoner do you want living next to you? No matter how you feel about the subject, the reality is that these prisoners are indeed coming home, and you do have the power to help shape what kind of neighbor they will be. Why education? Because it is the one science that overwhelmingly works.*

Based on more than a quarter century of teaching incarcerated students, I'd have to say that he's right. And many studies have shown that the more education a prisoner receives, the less likely he is to reoffend.

I assign Larry's essay every semester as required reading to on-campus students in my advanced literature class, which has the theme "crime and punishment." The class attracts a large number of criminology and psychology majors. Here's a typical example of what my students have to say about the essay:

> *Prior to reading this essay about correctional education, I had my own uneducated opinion of this topic. I believed, like many others in society, that prisoners did not deserve to have an education. They committed crimes, and they should be punished for them, not rewarded. However, my opinion about correctional education was shifted during my reading of "Doing Good for Bad Done." I now believe that correctional education is a great benefit for prisoners and for society. He makes a valid point. Providing prisoners with the opportunity to obtain an education could give them hope, help make themselves feel worthy and knowledgeable, and most importantly help them become a better person with a vision in life.*

From behind prison walls, Larry is reaching hundreds of students on campus and teaching them valuable lessons. The irony is that Larry himself will never be able to earn his own degree. In 2010, the state of Indiana revoked funding for correctional education.

Chapter 62

Correctional Education

The state of Indiana's decision to discontinue higher education for inmates closed a door in many lives—including my own. Not only had I taught college-credit courses to prisoners since I joined the faculty of Indiana State University in 1997, but also I had been appointed to an advisory position by the dean of the College of Arts and Sciences during the year that ISU expanded its prison degree programs from the two-year associate's degree to a four-year bachelor's degree. In coordination with the dean and associate dean, I created the bachelor's degree upper-division course curriculum.

"This is better than what students on campus take," my department chairperson had admitted.

I thought so too. Although I was not yet tenured, I had been appointed by the chairperson to serve as the director of undergraduate studies for the Department of English. In that capacity, I worked with hundreds of campus students in scheduling their classes, and I commonly saw seniors filling their final semester with fun courses to lighten their load or introductory-level courses they had neglected to take as freshmen. By contrast, prisoners took a full load (five or six classes per semester) of only 300- or 400-level courses. Furthermore, these were all upper-division advanced courses for which they had been prepared by their associate's degree curriculum. Finally, the courses formed a cohesive, themed focus for each semester, alternating between America and the world, classic and contemporary. One semester might include Classical Greek Mythology along with History of the Ancient World. The next semester might have Twentieth-Century American History along with Jazz Music or Modern Theater.

Because the courses were linked, the students were the same in each class and formed a cohort of "study buddies." Because they were the same students each semester, professors got to known them well and could consult with one another about their students' individual strengths and weaknesses. In these respects, the education that prisoners received was superior to that on campus. In other ways, of course, it was lacking: students and professors alike complained about the minimal availability of books and limited access to computer materials. Personally, I saw that as a plus: the Shakespeare text I assigned had no footnotes, nor could the students access Internet sites like SparkNotes that on-campus students often leaned on as a crutch. And, of course, there was no texting in class.

Yeah, I was gonna miss all that when I turned to teaching full-time on campus.

Chapter 63

"Cool!"

I saw you on TV last night!" one of my students on campus blurted out in the middle of my admittedly dry review of common grammatical errors in freshman writing. All heads turned away from me and to the girl in the back row.

"You was in *prison*!"

So much for grammar. That kind of "lecture interruptus" happened pretty frequently, at least once every semester, because the two MSNBC *Lockup* episodes that included a segment on my program aired frequently in reruns—most often at two in the morning, when my students should have been writing their papers, not watching prison documentaries. As soon as they heard the word "prison," the students' attention could not be easily returned to grammar. I had to take a little detour from the day's lesson to field the usual questions: Is there a guard in the classroom? (No.) Are you alone? (Yes.) Are you scared? (No.) After a brief description of what I did, they always concluded with a collective "*Cool!*"

The president thought my work was cool too. Not the president of the United States—the president of the university, which, to me, was much more important. President Dan Bradley and first lady Cheri Bradley attended one of the Shakespeare performances and, like everyone else, they were impressed with

Larry. A key component of the university's five-year strategic plan was community service, and I was providing it, along with excellent media coverage for the university. It couldn't hurt to have the president's support when I submitted my application for tenure—or so I thought.

"Service won't get you tenure," cautioned my colleagues in the English Department. It didn't matter how impressed the president was; he wouldn't even get to see my application if it was rejected by my department.

Reactions to my work in the department were as varied as the faculty in that large unit. Some of my colleagues sent me clippings of newspaper articles about my work, with collegial comments: "Great work, Laura!" Others expressed their views that prisoners don't deserve any kind of special treatment, educational or otherwise. Most of them were just too busy with their own work and, honestly, I was too.

My boss's publications included a highly respected five-hundred-page grammar manual, and even though he continued to be skeptical about prisoner rehabilitation and resentful of my hours spent on off-campus service work, he was growing impressed with Larry's own voracious appetite for knowledge—not just of Shakespeare, but grammar, too. Every week, in the middle of our Shakespeare work, Larry would throw out questions to me like, "Why's it called a semicolon?" Or "Does an acronym have to spell out another word, or can it just be initials?" With the prison's approval, my boss donated a copy of his book, personally inscribed, to Larry. When I presented it, Larry was visibly moved.

"Aw, man," he said. "This is such a big deal. Thank you. Thank him." He clutched the book in both his hands, hugging it, and added, "I'm going to read it—all of it!" And he did: all five hundred pages. All grammar.

Chapter 64

Timeline of Anxiety

Despite Larry's written response to the scene in which Macbeth murders King Duncan, the murder he was convicted of was the one topic that we never discussed. And I never asked. After visiting the scene of the crime, I had wanted to try to bring it up but never felt comfortable doing so, especially in front of the other prisoners.

We finally had that conversation years later, when he was no longer in segregation. We were sitting side-by-side, in an empty classroom in the general population area of the prison. No other prisoners were present. Not even a guard. Just me and Larry.

By then, I had rejected the idea of writing an article about Shakespeare. Instead, I was working on a book about Larry. His was the "silenced voice" I thought I would find in solitary confinement, and he did have something important to say. I began tape-recording our conversations with his permission (and the prison's). He agreed to talk openly about anything in his life—even, eventually, this.

He started to speak, then hesitated, bouncing his leg, drumming his fingers.

"Yeah, man, I don't know. I'm uncomfortable."

"Do you want me to turn off the recorder?"

"No, I don't mind that," he replied. "I just don't want *you* to..."

"To what?"

"To, I don't know, man, not *like* me anymore." He laughed nervously. I knew it was a difficult topic for him to relive and that he was using humor to deflect his discomfort.

"It's okay," I assured him. "Go on."

I felt relieved that he was not offended by my questions. Despite his displaying a good deal of hesitation, I was impressed with the candor with which he related his recollection of the events leading up to the murder. He described how nervous he had felt that night driving around with the others looking for trouble.

"I'm trying to remember the state I was in," he said sincerely. "What my thoughts were, how I felt."

He described the different levels of anxiety that come before, during, and after any criminal event. He referred to the stages as a "timeline of anxiety." He told me that he felt the same thing every time he stole a car or broke into a house—even when he stole that first ice cream cone as a kid.

"My heart and mind felt like—it's a bad analogy, but it's all I can think to describe that weird state—it was almost like being drunk at an exciting party. No, it's better described as hyperventilation. Sit in a chair and lean towards your knees, take fifty deep breaths quickly."

He started to demonstrate.

"After you stop—that is how you feel. You do have a presence of mind, but then again you don't. You're predominantly functioning on instinct. Up until the deed, you're choosing which primitive instinct to follow: fight or flight. At the deed, you're functioning on either one. So all of the logical behaviors you would expect from someone at this time are really unrealistic expectations."

That made sense to me, and it seemed like an important observation on the nature of criminal behavior: one that criminologists—and potential victims—need to know.

"I remember hoping that we would not find anyone out that night," he continued.

As I listened to him piecing the moments together, I tried to re-create the events in my mind: a group of teenagers driving around the dark Muncie streets in the early morning hours...a lone college student walking his girlfriend home... the treelined streets...the alley. The images were all clear in my mind. Too clear.

"After a while, it was starting to look like we would not find anyone out," Larry continued, "and I was really happy." He paused for a moment, and started to speak again with more difficulty. "But then...but then..."

But then the group spotted Christopher J. Coyle leaving a party, walking a female home—so that she would be safe. Newspaper accounts state that he was abducted, driven to an alley, robbed, and shot.

I didn't want to urge him to discuss the shooting. Instead, I wanted to learn more about his reaction.

"Tell me," I said softly, "more about the 'timeline of anxiety.' What were you feeling at that moment?"

"I remember having no control, no control of thoughts or anything like that. You're just kinda at the mercy," he replied. "That's the peak of the anxiety. Any more and I imagine a person would pass out."

Four teens ended up being charged in the shooting; however, when I read over the newspaper accounts, I found nothing that seemed to suggest—beyond the shadow of a doubt—which one had actually been the killer. Larry had entered a guilty plea in the courts, but was he really guilty? Given his psychological instability at that time, I wondered, could he even know?

"No matter what," Larry replied. "I feel responsible for the life of this man."

Finished, he looked at me for a reaction.

"That's good," I said, referring to the honesty, not the deed.

He nodded. "You know, this is the first time that I've really come face-to-face with this. I'm at the point now that I just have to surrender to the reality that this deed is, and will always be, a part of me. I will never be able to separate it from myself. But, *man*! What an ordeal!"

Unlike Macbeth, he had dared to "look on't again." Getting convicted killers to "look on" their deed again is an important step to keep them from killing again. That's precisely what we had been doing through our work all of these years.

I had one more question that I thought he would be able to answer.

"If this isn't too personal…?" I asked.

"Go ahead," Larry answered. "I mean, where else can we go?"

"Could the kid have done anything to save his life?"

"No," he replied immediately. "'Cause you're just kind of, not numb, but just…I don't know what. Numb. I don't know what other word to use."

"Nothing could reach you?"

"No." He thought for a bit, then added, "Well, it's so hard to say. You can't see anything else. You can't even ponder anything else. It's crazy, but it may be the clearest mind you'll ever have, there's no disruption, no thought coming in or nothing. You're not even thinking. You're just on this weird freakin' beeline kind of behavior, man! So I would say no for that reason. But maybe if the guy had a different behavior, then it would trigger a different behavior. Like, if there's another trigger, then yeah maybe I can see that."

"Did he try?"

"Not that I remember. See, this is the weird thing: I know

things were said, but I cannot tell you for the life of me what was said. I know things were said, 'cause I know that there's noise; when I'm back in the car and back in the moment, I know there's noise."

"What about leading up to that unreachable state? At that point—"

"Yes! The answer is yes. Can something trigger a different behavior? My thought is we'll jump out and start shooting, but him getting in the car changes my whole approach, so something can trigger a different kind of behavior."

"In other words, something surprising or unexpected could redirect you. So if the kid had done something unexpected—"

"Man! I wish he woulda!"

"You sound like Macbeth: 'Wake Duncan with thy knocking! I would thou couldst!'"

Chapter 65

Media Celebrity

It was the summer of 2008. With each passing year, the Shakespeare program was garnering more and more attention through local, national, and even international media stories. The prison's public relations director sent out announcements of all of our work and arranged for each interview. Each summer's performance of the play adaptations written by SHU prisoners made the front page of the local papers. "He did not even know who Shakespeare was," was the caption under a photo of Larry. The story was picked up by the Associated Press and reprinted in more papers than I could keep track of. National Public Radio did a lengthy feature story. MSNBC spent a full day with us, from which it created two segments for its *Lockup* and *Lockup Raw* programs. Even the international scholarly publication *The Chronicle of Higher Education* devoted its centerfold spread to our work: "Where Daggers Are Only of the Mind."

All of the coverage was glowing, showing both the prisoners and the prison in a positive light, recognizing the life-altering value of our work. "Indiana inmates drive home lessons from Shakespeare," read one Associated Press headline. "Inmates using the arts to send kids a message," read another. A front-page story in the local newspaper drew the attention of the lieutenant governor, who sent me a note saying, "I want to commend you for what you have accomplished with these inmates. It appears they have learned so much about life, choices, and control. Congratulations, and I look forward to hearing about many more people benefitting from your program."

We were often featured in the Department of Corrections website and publications as well, and I was even presented with the prison's Community Service Award given to its volunteer of the year. My mentor, Father Bob, quoted Shakespeare as he described the program to the audience at the awards ceremony: "The quality of mercy is not strained. It droppeth as the rain from heaven."

When the Discovery Channel, which had filmed the reenactment of the attempted escape from the SHU in 2000, started to plan its return visit to Wabash, the prison's media director told the producer to call me. On the phone from Australia, he asked me to tell him all about the Shakespeare program. He was the same producer who had done the reenactment of Larry's hostage attempt ten years earlier.

"Oh, wow!" he said when I told him that I was working with a prisoner who had spent ten years in isolation.

"Oh, wow!" he said when I told him that this prisoner was now the leader of the Shakespeare program.

"Oh, *wow!!*" he said when I told him that this same prisoner was the star of that earlier Discovery Channel episode. With his previous experience at the prison, the producer had a very good view of what a tremendous transformation Larry made. He determined that he wanted to plan an entire hour-long episode just on Larry and his work in the program.

Even Hollywood came to central Indiana. A couple of independent producers wanted to do a full-length feature film on the Shakespeare program with the focus on our greatest success story: Larry. As we escorted them out of the prison, after two full days of filming interviews with Larry, the assistant superintendent pulled me aside.

"Be careful," he warned me.

"Of what?" I asked.

"Jealousy."

A48 THE CHRONICLE OF HIGHER EDUCATION • OCTOBER 19, 2007

NOTES FROM ACADEME *By Peter Monaghan*

Where Daggers Are Only of the Mind

Bard behind bars

Shakespeare in prison

By ZACH HERMAN
Sentinel Staff Writer

A WAY TO ESCAPE

INMATES WRITE, PERFORM OWN VERSION OF 'MACBETH'

Tribune-Star/Joseph C. Garza

Their version: A program for "Shadows of Macbeth" sits near a pile of props before the play Friday at the Wabash Valley Correctional Facility near Carlisle.

Home > News > Story

Shakespeare lives on behind prison walls

Inmates act out

Wabash Valley Correctional Facility residents find outlet in Shakespearean tragedy "MacBeth"

Chapter 66

Cell Phone in the Cell

All good stories have unexpected plot twists, and this one is no different. It is not a linear tale of a bad man who, after reading Shakespeare for a few years, became a good man and did everything right for the rest of his life. True, Larry did everything right for several years: Almost immediately out of segregation, he was given the first job in his life, in the prison factory, and did so well that he was quickly promoted to line boss. As he promised, he enrolled in college and maintained a perfect 4.0 grade point average—the only prisoner I know to ever have done so. He sent his weekly paychecks home to his mom to put into a savings account for his graduate school tuition. And the Shakespeare workbooks he had written were being used by hundreds of students each year: in the SHU, in the prison's college classes, and even by my law-abiding on-campus students. (Having finally achieved tenure, I was teaching advanced undergraduate and graduate-level Shakespeare courses, using Larry's workbooks as the main textbooks.) And he was the star of all of the media interest. It was, in Larry's own words, "the best time of my life—without question!"

So, what happened? Was the pressure of so many successes, the first real successes in his life, too much? Was the jealousy of the prison population, whether inmates or officers, a factor?

Was he set up? In any case, just when he was at the top of his game came word that he was in trouble: a write-up.

"*A write-up?!*"

That was my reaction when the officer told me the reason Larry was not going to be able to come to our session that evening.

"Are you sure?" I asked, trying to peer over the desk at the paper that the officer was consulting. "Larry—I mean, Offender Newton—hasn't had a write-up in *four years*!"

The officer shrugged like it was no big deal, but it was: four years is a long time to be free of any kind of prison infraction. For Larry, it was the longest trouble-free time in his life.

I was stunned, but reassured to learn that, after Larry's early history of violent offenses, this incident was not violent. Nor was it a Class A offense. It was possession of a cell phone, the most popular infraction among prisoners: a Class B offense. It carried only a six-month "time out" in a disciplinary unit, after which the offender returned to general population with all of his privileges. But in Larry's case, he lost his job, his college career, his freedom, his phone calls, his family visits, and, above all else, his Shakespeare program—all this despite two full years of exemplary good conduct since his release from the SHU into general population, and two years free of infractions prior to that. At the most productive time in his life, he was suddenly put into an idle cell house, surrounded by prisoners serving disciplinary sentences. Even more than the SHU, it was, for him, a dangerous environment.

The next two years would bring Larry back to where he had been before Shakespeare: back to SHU...and back to the brink of suicide.

Chapter 67

Back to Seg

While Larry was sitting in G-house, the disciplinary unit, I was in the next building, the YIA unit. I was sitting with a group of those whom Larry called "kids in need," showing them our *Romeo and Juliet* adaptation called *Tybalt Must Die!* The video clearly captured the interest of these kids with short attention spans. Even better, those who declined our invitation to view our video in the cell-house dayroom were pressing their faces against the little windows in their cell doors, eager to see what was going on.

All of the top administration of the facility were in attendance, giving me enthusiastic greetings and glowing comments. Of course, there was media coverage as well, guaranteed to be favorable. A prison photographer was taking photos for the Department of Corrections website. It was a great day for the Shakespeare program, and Larry's leadership role really came through in the video. Each scene ended with him raising his challenging questions ("What is Tybalt really after in seeking Romeo's life? Is it murder—or is it something else?") that were designed to help these incarcerated teens turn away from their pattern of violence before they ended up like him, in prison for life.

"He's something, isn't he?" I said to the YIA manager.

"He's back in the SHU," he replied. "He was transferred this morning."

Why? There was no new write-up, not even a charge or a hearing. He was designated A/S (Administrative Segregation), despite having no apparent justification for segregated incarceration. Although it seemed unfair, I was at least relieved that he was out of the disciplinary cell house, because it was comprised solely of prisoners serving disciplinary time for a current offense, and, as such, Larry would be surrounded by some pretty negative peer pressure. Furthermore, I assumed that now that he was back on my original turf of the SHU, I would be able to see him at any time, that he would be able to lead the program there.

To my surprise, he was not allowed access to the program, nor was I allowed access to him. When I asked why, I was told that it was "confidential" information—something I had never been told about any prisoner before. Being only a volunteer at the facility, I had to accept that and recognize that—as Larry so often liked to say—"it is what it is." And so it was that Larry had to sit idle in his cell, even though he was just down the hall from my weekly segregated Shakespeare group. In fact, he was right back where I used to meet with him every week when I started the program six years prior.

Chapter 68

Remembering the Victims

Although he was sitting in a segregation cell, Larry's influence continued to guide the Shakespeare program: "This is not just a compilation of great stories," Larry had told the audience at the last performance. "It is a tool that we can use to change people's lives." As a follow-up to the *Romeo and Juliet* project, in which they used classic literature to try to help contemporary at-risk teens, the Shakespeare groups in population and in segregation wanted to reach out to another population in need. One member balked at the idea: "Aw, man," he said. "I'm sick of tragedy. Can't we do a comedy for a change?" Another member suggested they reach out to victims of crime, specifically women who have suffered from domestic violence. The choice was obvious: Shakespeare's comedy about domestic abuse, *The Taming of the Shrew*.

Larry's earlier workbooks asked prisoners to reflect on whether they feel remorse or regret for the crimes they have committed. Regret suggests a concern for yourself: "I'm sorry I got caught because I'm sorry I'm in prison," whereas remorse is driven by a concern for the victim: "I'm sorry I did that because I'm sorry he's dead." Or sorry that she's hurt.

When Larry was in the disciplinary cell house, prior to being transferred back to the SHU, I asked the superintendent to allow him to write another workbook, on *The Taming of the Shrew*. Larry dutifully submitted pages every week through the superintendent's office. True to form, he found great significance in passages often overlooked by scholars and theater professionals. Shakespeare's play opens with two short scenes that provide a framework for the play-within-a-play that is performed for the entertainment of a drunken bum who is literally picked up by a "lord" and made to believe he is, in fact, a wealthy man himself. These "induction" scenes are usually cut in performances of the play, and many scholars have found them to be meaningless distractions from the main plot.

Larry disagreed: "Arguably the most important element of this play is the Lord's social experiment! Do you remember the Eddie Murphy movie *Trading Places*? A couple of modern-day lords make a bet on whether or not a change in circumstances could change Murphy's tendencies. Would he return to a life of crime or excel in his new privileged life? That is what we have here, only four hundred years earlier. And the Lord is right! A person can be completely changed if the world around him is reshaped."

While Larry was writing the workbook, I was meeting with a group of incarcerated women who had been victims of domestic violence. They shared their stories, which I brought to the men in order to give them an understanding of this issue from the victim's perspective. The process began with me reading to the women a letter written by the men:

> Dear Sister,
>
> The abuse that you've experienced in your life was not your fault. You didn't deserve it. You don't deserve for any harm to ever come your way.... I just want you to know that I care. You are the essence of life, a

> harmonious display of nature's divine beauty. You are priceless and blessed. The struggles in life are nothing more than a test. After every dark night always comes a brighter day. We greatly appreciate you helping us to become better men during this process. We thank you for giving us a response to these very personal questions.

A list of twenty questions followed. Some of them were:

Which do you believe is worse: mental, physical, sexual, or psychological abuse?

"Mental," the women answer unanimously. "The pain from physical abuse heals."

What is love?

"Caring, respect, honesty. Listening, being there."

"Not hurting, not hitting, not molesting. Love is not pain."

"When two people can trust, depend on, and honor each other through all of life's trials and tribulations."

"I've never known it."

If you could change one thing about the men in your life, what would it be? (You can use extra paper, if you need it.)

"That they could love someone without hurting them."

"Their ability to listen.

"Talk things out instead of fighting."

"That he would learn to love himself and see his self worth."

What would you say if you felt safe enough to say it?

"I love you, but you are making me hate you."

"You are making me miserable, but I'm too scared to leave."

"Please see me as an equal. My feelings count."

"You need help."

"Bye!"

These dialogues continued, back and forth, for nearly a year. It was a powerful experience for both groups. The women felt like they were being heard for the first time, and the men were beginning to see how their actions have affected people in their own lives. They recalled the victims of their crimes, as well as the girlfriends, wives, mothers, and sisters they had hurt, whether physically or emotionally. Hearing from one another, through my mediated messages, both the women and the men working on this project often broke down in tears. I felt privileged to be permitted to observe such personal and profound experiences. I also felt fortunate, after listening to the most horrific stories of abuse, to be able to return home to my loving husband.

"This is a groundbreaking endeavor for the facility," the superintendent proudly told the media in an interview.

But as we prepared for the performance of the play adaptation that the men had written in collaboration with the women, anxieties among the members of the drama group ran deeper than usual. They were less focused, less disciplined than ever before. And nothing I could do seemed to help. I knew that what they needed was an internal leader, a peer who could motivate them like no outsider ever could. After several stressful weeks, one member voiced what had been on everyone's minds: "We need Larry."

Chapter 69
Full Circle

"Mr. Newton!"

I was standing outside of Larry's SHU cell, wearing a bulletproof vest to talk through a pegboard steel door with someone I had sat with alone in an unsupervised room for the past several years. It felt surreal. But I was pleased to see that he was not sleeping or watching TV, like most of his neighbors. He had his light on—and he was reading his Shakespeare book.

"Yes!" he replied, jumping up and coming to the cell door. One more time, I was impressed with his respectful demeanor toward the officer that he assumed was at his door, calling him by his last name. Instead, who he found standing on the other side of that familiar pegboard cell door was his Shakespeare professor.

"Oh, man," he said with a wide grin. "I don't believe you!"

We weren't permitted face-to-face sessions, and this brief "house call" was unofficial, but we were eventually allowed to have video visits, in which we communicated via real-time video hookup while sitting in two different areas of the SHU building. The assistant superintendent also encouraged us to continue our work through correspondence. I saw that as an opportunity for Larry not only to stay positively focused, but also to demonstrate to the administration that he was serious about this work and, in so doing, earn the right to return to the program. He was serious. He sent at least twenty pages every week, never missing a week.

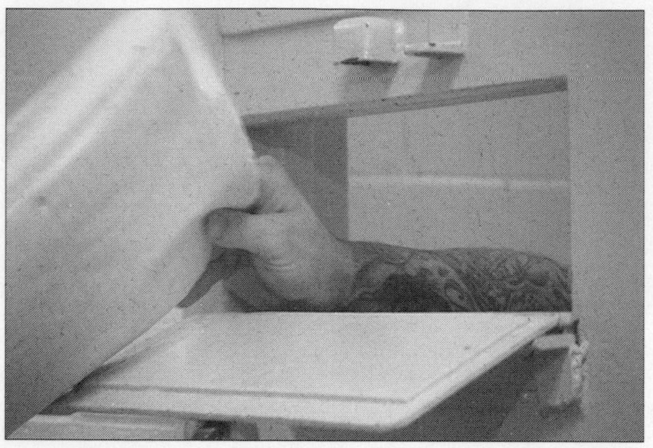

(Photo credit: Indiana State University)

Chapter 70

Tragic Kingdom

The cell phone was never proven to have been Larry's (his cell mate submitted a statement swearing that it had been his, not Larry's), but as a result of the possession charge, Larry spent six months in the disciplinary cell house in general population, while the Shakespeare group prepared their performance of *The Taming of the Shrew*. After that, he spent another six months in the SHU, without a conviction or even a hearing on any charge. He spent that time not sulking or fuming, but writing another workbook, the most ambitious of all, covering all nine of Shakespeare's history plays: *Richard the Second*; *Henry the Fourth Part One* and *Part Two*; *Henry the Fifth*; *Henry the Sixth Part One*, *Part Two,* and *Part Three*; *Richard the Third*; and *Henry the Eighth*. Arguably the most difficult plays in the collection, they are rarely read by students and infrequently examined by scholars. At sixty thousand words, Larry's workbook was longer than my PhD dissertation. And, in one important respect, it was also better. Doctoral dissertations are a composite of others' ideas, with footnoted material almost as long as the text itself. In Larry's work, all sixty thousand words represented his own original thinking on these plays, without the crutch of professional scholars' writing.

He began with the observation: "Sitting there on your bunk,

you may find it difficult to relate to a king sitting on a throne. But we are all the same people, just in different places."

Like King Richard the Second, imprisoned in a windowless concrete isolation cell, Larry sought to "people [his] little world" with his own thoughts, as he studied how he might compare kings from English history with his world of contemporary convicts. Imprisoned in isolation cells, the prisoners incarcerated in the nation's many segregated units were the intended audience for this book. Segregation can have detrimental psychological effects on the prisoner that can foster resentment and hostility that inspire further criminal activity. Or it can offer an unprecedented opportunity for intellectual activity, introspective reflection, and personal growth. Such positive outcomes could be further enhanced by the use of this workbook, written as an advanced course to follow our previous workbooks.

All of these books follow our mission to use the classic plays of Shakespeare to provide incarcerated—and most especially, segregated—readers with an intellectual exercise that can also raise life-changing questions. As readers engage in an analysis of Shakespeare's characters, they cannot help but engage in an analysis of their own character, motivations, and objectives. In this advanced course, we challenged the reader with deeper questions that examined the very core character of a man, whether he is a king or a convict; questions that could indeed change a prisoner's life—even while he is incarcerated in a windowless concrete isolation cell.

King Richard the Second relates to prisoners in several ways, beginning with his obvious uncanny depiction of a supermax solitude. Of great interest also is when Richard says, "Throw away respect, tradition, form and ceremonious duty, for you have but mistook me all this while: I live with bread like you, feel want, taste grief, need friends: subjected thus, how can you say to me I

> *am a king?" It is that relation to normal that we need to restore in the convict! The convict may not sit on a throne, but he shares the same affliction with Richard. Everyone treats Richard as a king, until he is no longer Richard. He sees himself as nothing but the role, the position. The convict eventually loses himself as well and becomes nothing but the role, the position. Everyone treats the convict as a monster, until even he eventually accepts that he is a monster. But underneath is still the innate human desire to be normal. Convicts need to understand that they are not their deeds! They are not the roles that they are playing! They do not need to be defined by others' perceptions. The best of men—kings—share the same human qualities with us.*
>
> Richard the Second *is our launching pad that brings convicts back to normalcy. Then we break the curse that they are defined by their deeds with* Henry the Fourth. *After that, we build in them the potential for greatness with* Henry the Fifth. *In* Henry the Sixth, *we teach them to keep that potential grounded in realistic options. And with* Richard the Third, *we show them that it is essential that they follow their intrinsic motivations. Richard the Third is the consequence of not being rewarded as one thinks he should be. He is the consequence of extrinsic motivation. We do not live in fantasy worlds, and adversity will always exist, especially when one has a history such as ours, but when we are intrinsically driven, as Henry the Eighth is, the adversities do not have breaking power!*

Larry's interpretation of Shakespeare's villain king is most startling of all:

> *There is no mistaking that Richard the Third is a wicked man, but Richard is the rarest form of wicked because he simply wants to be loved!! Sound crazy? Well, it is, and it makes Richard one of Shakespeare's most complicated characters. Long before the FBI*

or any of the great social scientists, Shakespeare understood the environment most productive to create a killer! Richard devoted himself, and spilled his blood, to make his brother king. And what has it all done for him? Nothing! He is still the monster of England! He is still a mere "crookback"! He is still shown no respect, no admiration, hell—no love, whatsoever! Until this very moment this man has been nothing less than a great son, a great brother, a great soldier, a great citizen, a great patriot—but not a single one of these qualities is identified with him. Instead, he is merely a crookback cursed by god to harvest evil. Well, if you tell a man he is something for long enough, he will become that. I was told all of my life that I would end up in prison—and sure enough, I did not disappoint.

Richard has not given in to the suggestion that he is less than he wants to be, but we all have breaking points. Like Hamlet, Richard's father has suffered a great dishonor, and just as the ghost of Hamlet's father obligated Hamlet to revenge his dishonor, Richard's father has obligated him to revenge: "My ashes, as the phoenix, may bring forth a bird that will revenge upon you all." He was bred for revenge! Once he has revenged his father and his family, what is left for him? That's right: to revenge his own dishonors. Who's to blame for them? Yes, everyone!! How can you expect a man cultured for revenge not to revenge? The world has created him, and the world will suffer his revenge. The moral of Richard's story is not to identify other Richards before they happen, but rather that inhumanity will only create greater inhumanity. Am I supposed to feel sympathy for what Richard will do for England? Well, I feel sympathy for what England has done to Richard!

The workbook concludes with a final consideration:

After our long investment in these plays, let's not overlook how these kings compare to us. We are not monsters, and we are not saints, and yet we are both. We are much more similar to Henry the Eighth and like him we have to find a balance between satisfying our selfish impulses and considering the footprints we leave in other peoples' lives. The world does not belong to us, and we have to figure out how to enjoy it within the confines of a society, if we are not doomed to continue reliving the nightmares that we have been. Much as Henry did regarding his marriage, we need to get sick of the "same ol' thing." The main question to leave this study with is: What will it take to get you to drag yourself out of your grave?

The history plays workbook was truly a remarkable achievement, undertaken in the most challenging of conditions.

And then, conditions got worse.

(Photo credit: Indiana State University)

Chapter 71

"Stay Strong"

I arrived at the prison on an especially cold and blustery day in January of 2010. Walking across the snow-covered prison yard toward the SHU building, it occurred to me that I was about to begin my second decade in solitary confinement. When would this ever end? How would it end? For the time being, I brushed those thoughts aside. I knew that we still had work to do—important work.

I was expecting to have another video visit with Larry, as arranged by the assistant superintendent. At his request, Larry and I were preparing an entirely new program that would bring Shakespeare to the most difficult population in the prison: the SNU (Special Needs Unit). The criminally insane. The one unit that my husband—and even Larry—cautioned me about. Despite their concerns, I was optimistic. I took a full day off from my campus commitments to meet with the director of the SNU, as well as the officers and psychiatrists and even some of the prisoners of the unit. Everyone enthused about the materials that Larry and I had developed thus far. They were so committed to our impending program that they had posted an announcement and sign-up sheet in the cell house. Even though I had to admit that working in that unit would be risky, I felt confident that this monumental endeavor, undertaken on behalf of the facility, would finally earn Larry the right to return to general population.

So imagine my surprise when I arrived at the SHU and the secretary informed me that "Offender Newton was transferred."

I might have asked, "When?" I should have asked, "Why?" Instead, I asked, "To *where*?"

Larry believed that he would never be sent back to the other supermax at Westville Correctional Facility in Michigan City because of his two escape attempts. But he was. Again I asked why, and again I was told that the information was "confidential." As an outsider, I cannot assume to understand the complex workings of the criminal justice system, but it did strike me as risky to send a prisoner back to a facility from which he had had two successful escape attempts. Furthermore, the unit manager who had been in charge during his escape attempts of twelve years earlier was snatched up from his position downstate and sent back to Westville. What kind of treatment could Larry expect in his hands? This manager knew nothing of our Shakespeare program or of the good work that Larry had done for the past eight years. He knew only what a problem Larry had been twelve years ago, and this was his long-awaited chance for revenge—ironically, to be inflicted on the very prisoner who had spent years turning prisoners away from their impulses toward revenge!

Week after week passed, with no word from Larry. The secretaries at the university searched the campus mail every day for a letter. Good hearts, they prayed for him. Even my boss worried, "If they take away his Shakespeare book, he'll snap," he said. His scenario was plausible, but it sure wasn't reassuring.

"Stay strong" were Larry's parting words to me every week. I just had to trust that Larry was as strong—and as changed—as I believed he was.

Chapter 72
Closing Doors

Something seemed wrong. The prisoners seemed distracted. They kept casting furtive glances down the hall through the window in our classroom door. On a typical day, we would see a prisoner now and then walking to the chapel or infirmary, both of which were located here in the OSB (Offender Services Building). There was no officer in our room, but if one happened to be heading for the break room for a few minutes away from his post at the end of the hall, he might wave as he passed by. I started to realize that it was strange that I hadn't seen anyone out there for a while: no prisoners, no officers, no one. This was not a typical day. I was starting to feel something I'd never felt in prison before: fear.

The Shakespeare group stayed focused on the hallway, without saying why. Suddenly, it hit me: there was a fight taking place in the hall, apparently involving a couple of prisoners. It didn't involve any of our group members, but one of them must have had a vested interest in the outcome, because he got up and headed for the door.

"Don't hurt anyone," I begged him.

"Don't worry," he replied, "I won't."

But I knew he was only telling me what I wanted to hear. I assumed that the officers down the hall would stop him and send him back into the classroom, but he never returned. It was like he just vanished.

The group stopped talking about Shakespeare; in fact, they stopped talking altogether. Eventually, the silence was shattered by a siren that began blaring, something I'd never heard before. Before I could ask the group what to do, an officer appeared and ordered the prisoners out: *now!*

I gathered up my papers and threw them into my bag, grabbed my coat, and started to follow the prisoners toward the front door that leads out of the building. But the officer blocked my way and pointed in another direction without saying a word. I started to say to him, "That's not the way I usually go out," but he disappeared. I started down the unfamiliar corridors, through a door that I assumed would lead me out, but it didn't. In fact, it led me deeper into the prison. I was no longer in the safe confines of the OSB, but inside one of the cell houses. That sure didn't seem like a way out. I turned to go back, but the door wouldn't open! It was locked! I was in there alone, and I could not find my way out!

Desperately, I continued on past rows and rows and rows of cells. Not the familiar steel pegboard cell doors, but old-fashioned iron bars. I'd never seen cells that looked like that. Prisoners I didn't know looked scary—as "my" guys probably did to those who didn't know them.

"Don't worry," I told myself. "They're behind bars." And then...the bars opened, and one after another, prisoners came charging out of their cells, waving a variety of homemade weapons. It was turning into a full-fledged prison riot! Was I going to end up a hostage? This couldn't be happening!

It wasn't.

It was just a bad dream, the kind that I often have to this day. I never felt worried when I was in the prison, never had nightmares about working there when I was still working there, but maybe now my subconscious worries are surfacing. My sister tells me she's had similar nightmares about living in the 'hood—but, likewise, only after we no longer lived there.

I went back to the SHU one time after Larry was transferred, when I was no longer working there, and I was struck by the gates, the bars, the security—the risk. Although I'd only been away for a matter of months, I felt like I was seeing it all anew. The thought flashed in my mind: I can't believe I used to work back here! That I spent roughly one thousand hours here, entered this unit nearly five hundred times!

It might have been risky; I might have been crazy. But I'm glad I went in there, and that I also did, in the words of Dave Matthews, "find my own way out."

Chapter 73
The Letter

Finally, a letter arrived from Larry. The secretaries called me and I ran down the hall, as I had done eight years earlier when I had received permission to enter the SHU. I opened the letter in front of the assembled group, with no need for censorship. Breathlessly, I read aloud:

Dear Dr. Bates,

Hey you!

What a ride!

It was a rough one. King Richard's psychological state made physical. The day I arrived here (two weeks ago) the prison went on a weeklong lockdown to conduct facility-wide shakedowns. Brutal shakedowns! As a consequence of the lockdown I was held in a disciplinary observation cell for the week. In non-institutional talk that is a cell reserved for strapping a grown man to the bunk by his hands and feet. Like being buried alive I imagine. Included is a camera to observe the "disruptive" prisoner. The problem for me was that the cell is not meant to be lived in. That means that the cell never gets cleaned.

> With absolutely no property for me to clean the blood-stained walls and floor, I could survive still. What drove me nuts was—

"Oh, no!"

"What is it?" asked Mary Ann, one of the secretaries.

Recalling his one phobia, I continued reading the letter:

> What drove me nuts was the spiders, and their webs!! These webs were the stuff of legends. No angle was spared. I hate spiders! Not an animal I can trust. So I spent the week in the exact same spot—middle of the bed! I just sat there wondering how many tortured souls escaped right there on that bed. I wondered how many people were humanely put down unintentionally on that bed. My anger never has much of a life these days, but this adverse time chased it away rather quickly. I just felt sad. Not for myself, but for the men who helplessly stared at that ceiling, having no idea how to change! It sucked! The spiders were fitting: life just being sucked out of people. I never learned to pacify violence from violence, and these men will never shake a criminal impulse from criminal acts! A cycle with too many investors to be broken. Anyhow, the lockdown ended and I moved to a regular/normal supermax dungeon. Last night I received a letter from you that was sent to Wabash, and today I received my property. I am now normalized! So, here is my plan: I will finish organizing my property tonight, tomorrow I will attempt to recapture my Shakespeare momentum, this weekend I will sit down and respond to your letter, and include what work I was able to piece together. I should be able to recapture the mood in a day, two

> max. I feel like I miss you already, but nothing has really changed but my dungeon. It sure feels like a month at minimum. I just wanted to shoot you this quick "kite" since I received my property today, mainly to let you know that I am okay. I hope you are well. Stay strong!! I will!
>
> Always,
> Larry

"Whew!" was the collective response of my colleagues. I was grateful for their empathy, though I knew that they could not begin to imagine the conditions that Larry described. Even after spending nearly a decade in the "hole" myself, I couldn't imagine it.

I felt a mix of emotions: worried about Larry—and worried that it was my fault that he was in this situation. If it was true that I had saved his life, then had my well-intentioned efforts now endangered it? If only I had listened to my boss, had never entered the SHU, never met a prisoner named Larry Newton, never asked him to read Shakespeare, then he wouldn't have excelled in the program and been released from segregation, gone into general population, and had access to a cell phone....

I spent the next week worried sick. Literally, sick: sleepless nights resulting in elevated heart rate and blood pressure approaching dangerously high levels. I felt precisely the kind of worries that would have made my own mother heartsick too, if I had told her about my prison work.

CHAPTER 74

Powering through with Shakespeare

As promised, a second letter arrived the following week. It was written in journal style, with an entry for every day of the week—almost every day.

2-10-10

Dear Dr. Bates,

Hey you, how you is?

It is roughly 8 a.m., and I am about to attempt to recapture some Shakespeare mood. I thought I would go ahead and begin my letter first though. I am sitting in front of my window listening to the radio. My energy is building as I jam. I have a window here, and outside I see a ground covered in snow—deep snow! My entire horizon is the building itself, but since I am upstairs I can see over the building and see a highway in the distance. I cannot make out much, but at night I can clearly see the lights of the traffic, and it is nearly as intimate as an up-close. I squeeze my brain to picture myself behind the wheel, anticipating some destination. It is cool for me to know that these people are going somewhere. I love it!

No question about it, I am most intrigued by how other people live their lives. Even in pictures, my favorite sort is an un-posed moment! I can nearly live the moment myself. I can stare at one of those for hours. Man, it has been many years since I received any pictures. My mom used to take some for me, as did my brothers, but as time passes it must be less fun for them. I am promised many each year, but I would estimate it has been at least seven or eight years. In fact, I have no idea how long it has been!

Strangely, such a condition gives me some small exposure to my place in the world. If not for the biological obligation, I could be long passed to my outside world. I do not mean that in the tone it gives; I just mean that I really am more memory than an active member. Who would ever even know I existed, but my victims? The family of that poor guy, my family, and you guys (my only nonvictims). Beyond that: what footprint is there? That is a crazy thought, no? It sounds sinister, but I am not in a darkened mood. If anything, I just wonder how I can leave some footprints in the world. Probably a mortal complex that comes with not leaving any children. I did suddenly feel isolated though. Only briefly.

So, let's check out your letter.

I had written to him my enthusiastic response to his last letter, as well as a plea for him to stay on track, to keep on working.

I needed that by the way. It hit the spot, at the right time.

There was no end to the sentence, and no entry for the next day. The letter resumed one day later:

2-12-10

So much for normalized! I was pulled mid-sentence and strip-searched, all my property searched, and moved to yet another cell. The man who runs the place came and told me to blame him and not his staff. He said my name slipped by him at first, but suddenly he remembered me and the attempted escape of twelve years ago. Said I was the reason they brought him back. Assured me though that it was nothing "personal," and certainly not "harassment," but let me know that this will be a regular thing. To add insult, the new cell was another neglected dungeon! It took me four hours to clean it up, once I finally got in here. I am to expect shakedowns every day, and moving to a new cell every three days! I have done that before, but never for long-term. It is crazy! It stirs every unstable emotion in you, but worst of all it creates an intense paranoia. Every time you hear the range door, you tense up for another round of "not personal" security. It is not good! It is one thing to do it short-term, but something all together different for the long haul. You cannot settle anywhere! You cannot develop any relationships. You are on guard 24/7! I am lost right now. I have no idea what to do! I did nothing to get here, and most certainly did not ask for this. If I am really that much of an issue, then what sense does it make to put me here? This is going to be rough! That aside, let me tell you this story: Late last night, after cleaning this dungeon, I got to talk to someone here who did the Shakespeare program in the SHU! He just told me how great it was, and all of my grave concerns nearly vanished! He said at first he was skeptical, but he really got into it. I have yet to do my normal puzzle for troubles: that is, find some way that my problems are fated for my development, but I am certain that I cannot lay this work aside! In fact, this is a time for me to lean on Shakespeare! There is nothing else for me, except to fold to the negative energy thrown at me. No question, this is going to be a terrible experience, but if I can power through with Shakespeare—imagine the stability! So I will not let them take it from me: how about that?

2-13-10

They are shaking me down twice each day (once each shift), and with the moving around—it is harassment. I am trying to put together a letter to the commissioner that includes all of the great work reviews I received, as well as the great annual reviews I received. In fact, I never received a bad one! I need to show them that despite my one fumble, all of my reviews at each prison were great! Not good—great! To show basically that I am not some problem prisoner deserving of these conditions reserved for such a prisoner.

2-14-10

Rough day! Really rough day! I will make it okay. Will have plenty of work for you by next week, I promise. Actually, I need it right now. Anyhow, you are the best. I will not let you down! Trust me, my friendship with you has long motivated me more than Shakespeare ever did, and the last thing I would ever want is to let you down. You are, literally, my only friend, and that is never lost on me! Let me get this letter out. I feel so much better after I talk with you! Always do! Be easy, stay strong, and you young'uns have a great Valentine's Day.

Larry

And then nothing. For weeks. And nothing that I could do but worry again. Every one of the prison arts volunteers that I had become acquainted with over the years cautioned me that any attempt on my part to "advocate" for him would backfire. It would bring more attention to him and would likely make the prison administration come to regard him as a problem prisoner just when he needed to demonstrate that he was, in fact, a model prisoner. Again, I had to trust that Larry would come through, that he would do what he always told me to do: "stay strong."

Chapter 75
Revelation

Finally, the long-awaited letter arrived. It started with a confession—and ended with a revelation:

> My brain has been occupied with old demons, and I have been completely unable to focus on anything else. I have been in six different cells in the four weeks here! I have been shaken down roughly sixty times! I get it twice daily–no grandiosity! I get shook down once in the morning, and once at night–EVERY DAY! I am clean, and it should be no big deal, but it is not that simple. First there are the psychological consequences: it keeps me anticipating harassment all day. That is as distractive as a drug addict awaiting his next lick. The moving keeps me isolated socially, and that creates a depressed mood...after each shakedown, I spend at least an hour putting my legal work, and all paperwork, back in order. Every new cell takes me roughly eight hours of scrubbing to clean. The theme is obviously frustration. I feel absolutely violated and grossly persecuted! It is illegal and completely personal!

By the end of the letter, he was back to his optimistic mood:

> I moved again last night, but honestly I dealt with it much better. I stayed up until 3 a.m. cleaning the cell. But as is so common a coping mechanism: it is what it is. I am not at all discouraged! This is an entirely new student, with an entirely new appreciation for our work. Obstacles are a part of this beast, and one should always anticipate a climb. But as long as we stay strong on what we do, time will take care of the rest.

As my boss had feared, they did take his Shakespeare book, the one possession that meant the most to him—but he kept on working. Along with the letter, he sent twelve pages of work.

"Good man," said Mary Ann.

I wondered if Larry had ever been called that. And I wondered if Mary Ann had ever called another convicted killer that.

Now, the revelation:

> There is some good news, though: I just saved a bunch of money by switching to GEICO. No, but I did uncover an important answer to one of the most serious questions you have ever asked me! Remind me to answer you again, when we meet face-to-face. This is certainly not the media for it. But I can now tell you how I know. Maybe that was the point of this journey. None the less, I am in for one heck of a fight! Or maybe it is merely a better platform to prove myself? Maybe it is my chance to become Henry the Fifth? It would be one heck of a contrast!
>
> I am just unwilling to justify my stay here by obnoxious behavior. I just do not have it in me anymore. Believe me, I felt every bit of the pain, but you would never be able to tell it by watching me. I still conducted myself with respect—very dignified. No officer here will

> have a bad thing to say about me. I really am a different creature, even in my life away from you. I feel it all, and probably express the desperation, but it is not reflected in my conduct. In fact, that is how I discovered the answer to your question. You see, I attempted to conjure up the heart for a real-felt "fantasy," but I could not do it! I will explain one day....

He didn't have to explain; it had been my greatest worry during the past weeks. The letter ended with the following words:

> The answer is *no*, I will never kill again.

CHAPTER 76

Footprint in the World

While serving out an additional year in segregation, Larry completed his ultimate accomplishment, our final workbook: *The Prisoner's Guide to the Complete Works of Shakespeare.* In his introduction, Larry paints a powerful portrait of the conditions in which his work was undertaken:

> *Studying Shakespeare is inherently difficult. Studying Shakespeare in prison's supermax dungeons is just absurd! Imagine sitting at a metal desk in the middle of a sanitarium and opening up a Shakespeare book for the very first time. It is a bizarre contrast to hear the language of a tormented convict, as you are reading the English of old. Now just imagine the people all around you are at war with each other and with themselves, the sound of bodily waste hitting the range is constant, and the stench of that raw sewage is so strong that masking agents only complement the discomfort, water from the toilets is flooding the range at your feet, and everyone is screaming out of torment or fear or anger or sheer insanity. While you sit in the middle of this storm and try to figure out how Macbeth drove himself crazy.*
>
> *These are just the physical distractions competing for your attention. Mind you, the answers are all around you, if you can discipline your mind to break away from the insanity of the*

> *sanitarium and go into the insanity of the play. And transitions are the heart of our Shakespearean efforts! It is, after all, the bottom line. Fact is, you do not need me to tell you that the plays are excellent stories; they have been so for four hundred years. You do not need me to tell you how "deep" Shakespeare is; he has frustrated the greatest minds on the planet. What I can tell you is that ANY serious reader of Shakespeare is going to experience an evolution!*
>
> *It is an absolute magic, and the magic has little to do with what Shakespeare has to say. You can memorize every cool quote and be as clueless as you were before reading. So it is not Shakespeare's offering that invokes this evolution. The secret, the magic, is YOU! Shakespeare has created an environment that allows for genuine development. The Shakespearean efforts are not to replace your pre-existing ideas with the ideas of some facilitator. The efforts are not to see you become the cookie-cutter copy of what some other person thinks you "should" be.*
>
> *Shakespeare is simply an environment that allows us to evolve without the influence of everyone else telling us what we should evolve into. Shakespeare offers a freedom from those prisons! Your mind will begin shaking the residue of other people's ideas and begin developing understandings that are genuinely yours! That is the goal of these Shakespearean efforts. You have nothing to lose but the parts of you that do not belong anyhow.*

The introduction ends with the characteristic ☺.

Following this opening essay, each of the thirty-eight plays is given its own introduction of approximately one thousand words, just enough to clarify the plot, themes, and major characters. More importantly, these introductions help to put the new reader at ease, written in Larry's signature down-to-earth style, often making incongruous contemporary cultural connections.

For example:

Comparing *King Lear* to *The Waltons*:

Those of us who remember The Waltons *remember tuning in each week to witness a family struggling with some issue. The show was fulfilling because at its conclusion we witnessed compromise and understanding. The show ran parallel to our own convictions that no issue had the power to threaten our family bond. We all eagerly anticipated the show's conclusion, which was the family wishing each other a good night. The same conclusion each week, and yet we did not change the channel until we heard the "good night."* King Lear *will remind you of* The Waltons *a great deal, in that there is a family. But all comparisons end there!*

Comparing *Titus Andronicus* to *Mister Rogers' Neighborhood*:

I've heard it argued that television has become too violent. After reading this play, I would argue that the level of violence in our modern entertainment industry is about as comparable to this play as the children's show Mister Roger's Neighborhood *is to* Mortal Kombat. *I would not in any way argue for justification, but only that the level of violence has not increased, but rather it is relatively mild when compared to this four hundred-year-old play. How does one even summarize the gruesome behavior? Let's just say that Titus is a Roman general, who is in every respect a hero of Rome. He is so popular that the public wants him to fill the seat of the recently vacant emperor. He declines and gives his vote to one Saturninus. Titus has just returned from war with the Goths and has brought as a Roman conquest the queen of the Goths and her sons. To make a long story short, the new emperor Saturninus takes Tamora, Queen of the Goths, as his new wife. She gives a brand new meaning to "Hell hath no fury like a woman scorned"!*

Comparing *The Taming of the Shrew* to *The Honeymooners*:

> *"O Romeo, Romeo! Wherefore art thou Romeo?" Well, not quite. It is more like, "To the moon, Alice!" In this case, however, ole Ralph Kramden is not making hollow threats. He is attempting to "tame" a shrew of a lady by way of starvation, sleep deprivation, and bursts of sheer lunacy! Our Ralph Kramden is actually Petruchio, who is by all accounts on the hunt for some money, when he is approached with an opportunity to get a substantial amount of just that by a group of guys who are attempting to court the beautiful daughter of Baptista. Her name is Bianca, and she has an elder sister named Katherina, aka "Kate"—the bitter shrew of this story.*

And my personal favorite, comparing *The Winter's Tale* to *Frosty the Snowman*:

> *Do you remember the story of* Frosty the Snowman*? If you can recall, this jolly old fellow was slowly melting away as winter drew to a close. Remember? Well, that has nothing to do with this story.* ☺ *No, this is a nice little comedy about a man who goes insane from jealousy and kills his wife and kid. A real knee-slapper! Of course, there is nothing funny about the story, and "comedy" should not lead you to anticipate a chuckle. Today, "comedy" is pigeonholed to mean only one thing: humor. It was not always so. In Shakespeare's time, "comedy" had the diversity to make you laugh or make you cry.*

From cartoon characters, he moves on to German philosophers, as he points out that:

> A Midsummer Night's Dream *is no dream at all. This is a story about love, but a story that strips down some of the legendary*

> *ornamentation of love. Love from a distance looks like a blinding light, a single entity. This play filters that light and exposes love for what it really is: a passion! Nietzsche says, "All passions have a time when they are fate only, when with the weight of their folly they drag their victim down, and they have a later very much later period when they wed with spirit." How can love drag you down? Well, it's not love's doing. You have a primal instinct to eat, but if that impulse stood alone, void of judgment and responsible approaches, you are vulnerable to eating poisoned berries. Love alone has the same lacking of intentions. Love has no ambition—it just is. How we apply or understand these basic impulses will determine whether we poison ourselves or live long healthy lives.*

It is the culmination of our ten years' work, and it is a remarkable "footprint" for Larry to leave the world.

Chapter 77

Mother's Day

Time for my own confession—and my revelation. Just once, several years earlier, Larry had tried his best to get me to break my "no personal questions" rule. I had told him that I would not be at the prison the following week, that I was taking a week off.

"Must be something important," he surmised.

As I shrugged, he continued sleuthing.

"You're going out of town probably."

No response, which he took as a yes.

"Well, tell me this: are you leaving on a week*day* or a week*end*?"

I laughed. Such determination had to be rewarded.

"Family reunion," I said. It was like telling a kid that I was going to Disneyland. Actually, Larry reacted as if *he* were going to Disneyland.

"Family reunion!" he slapped the table with his palm. "Oh, man, that's awesome! I love family reunions!"

Have you ever felt that kind of reaction to the idea of rescheduling a chunk of your life to drive hundreds of miles to stay in a "kid-friendly" water park? Well, like so many other aspects of life, Larry had me seriously reconsidering what our annual family reunions meant to me. And more…

I knew better than to give any information about my family

to any prisoner, even Larry. I never told him where my sister lived, or how old my grandkids were, for example. All I told him was that our reunion involved the monumental task of assembling "our nineteen kids and grandkids."

"Oh, man, that's awesome!" he repeated. Then he looked at me thoughtfully and asked, "Do you think you're a good mother?"

No response. It was, after all, a personal question.

He answered it himself: "I think you are."

"No personal questions" was not the reason that I had not answered his question. What he didn't know was that I had nineteen *step*-kids and grandkids. That he was my only "child"—the only human being for whose life I could claim any kind of responsibility.

Or maybe he did somehow know because, from the Westville supermax, he sent me a Mother's Day card.

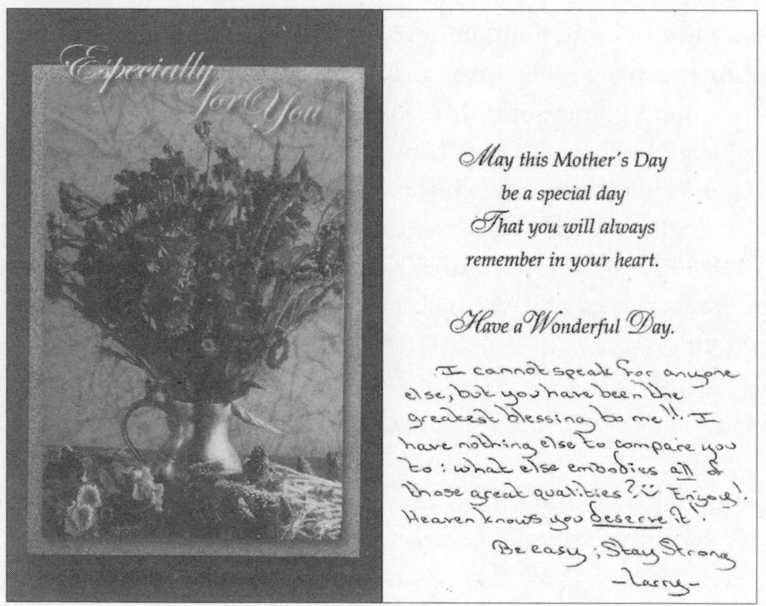

Chapter 78
Five Steps

One, two, three, four, five." I counted it out silently, with Larry's words ringing in my head, and the image of him pacing in his cell.

"Six, seven, eight, nine, ten," I continued, long after he would've hit a concrete wall.

"Eleven, twelve, thirteen, fourteen, fifteen." The sand was warm under my bare feet and soft, until I stumbled on a hard stone and recalled Larry's cold concrete floor.

"Sixteen, seventeen, eighteen, nineteen, twenty." The waves lapped rhythmically against the shore, a soothing accompaniment to my walk. Somewhere a dog barked and kids squealed, still more soothing than the tormented cries of the criminally insane.

"Twenty-one, twenty-two, twenty-three, twenty-four, twenty-five." The afternoon summer sky was a blend of bright blues dappled with shifting cloud patterns that resembled first a bird and then a butterfly, while Larry envisioned his own images in the unchanging gray of his concrete ceiling.

"Twenty-six, twenty-seven, twenty-eight, twenty-nine, thirty." The faintly fishy smell of the lake water, a healthier scent than the overflowing toilets on the range.

"Thirty-one, thirty-two, thirty-three, thirty-four, thirty-five." Burgers sizzled on a nearby grill, while officers shoved food through the slots in the steel cell doors.

"Thirty-six, thirty-seven, thirty-eight, thirty-nine, forty." I took a sip of cold beer, wondering when Larry last tasted a beer, and suddenly even a Bud Light tasted pretty good.

"Forty-one, forty-two, forty-three, forty-four, forty-five." The little beachfront harbor was full of colorful sailboats, motorboats, pontoon boats—real boats, not the fantasy boats that sailed in Larry's cell.

"Forty-six, forty-seven, forty-eight, forty-nine...*fifty*." In less than one minute, I had walked a distance ten times the size of Larry's world. I stopped in front of a pontoon boat moored at the dock.

After spending more than ten years in supermax segregation, Larry finally has broken out of his prison. Not the prison of concrete and steel, but the prison of self-destructive ways of thinking: "the only prison that matters."

Spending ten years in supermax myself taught me to recognize that Larry was right: despite having the liberty that he will never have, we all put ourselves into "so many prisons."

So now, to break out of one of my own, I took my husband's hand and climbed aboard.

Hey, you know what?

What if this was Paris? They have them outside tables and stuff.

And we was having coffee. And you had to go over there and grab you a donut or something. When you was going over there, would you grab your purse? Like, are you always aware that I'm a prisoner? You know what I mean? And I don't mean anything funny by that; I'm not going personal or anything. When I see pictures of myself, I think I look like a hardened criminal. I really do. So I just wonder, what do people think about me? What kind of person do they think I am? Because so many bad things are related to me. I don't think there's any way to avoid that reality. Okay, I'm here in my life now, but I still carry the weight of all this other stuff. So because that's true, I always wonder: How do you see me?

Do you see me as this guy carrying all these chains?

Or do you just see the chains?

(Photo credit: Jon Mac Media)

Afterword

Larry spent more than a year in the Westville supermax, completing a mandatory behavior-modification program that he had already completed at the SHU, in order to earn the right to return to population again. He was never charged with any disciplinary infractions to justify his segregation, and his conduct reports there were unanimously positive, so he was eventually returned to general population at Wabash. However, he was not permitted to return to the Shakespeare program. Nor was he able to return to his college career because, while he was in segregation, the Indiana state legislature revoked funding for higher education in prison; college classes are no longer offered in Indiana prisons.

With Larry's departure, I suspended the Shakespeare program at Wabash but helped to start offshoots of the program in other Indiana prisons, as well as in the long-term disciplinary segregation unit of the federal penitentiary: the federal "SHU."

While Larry's example inspires new programs across the state and across the nation, I am compiling his writings on all thirty-eight of Shakespeare's plays into *The Prisoner's Guide to the Complete Works of Shakespeare*.

That is, after all, his "footprint in the world."

Reading Group Guide

1. The U.S. Supreme Court is currently debating the constitutionality of capital punishment and life without parole for juvenile offenders. What is your opinion? Do you think that Larry, who came to prison at seventeen, should spend the rest of his life behind bars?

2. What kinds of conditions are appropriate for violent offenders? Do you agree that long-term solitary confinement is, as judged by Human Rights Watch, inhumane? What about solitary confinement for juveniles, as Larry experienced starting at the age of ten, described in Chapter 15 ("Supermax Kid")?

3. Is rehabilitation possible? What evidence can prove a prisoner's rehabilitation? Do you think Larry is rehabilitated?

4. Research has shown that higher education results in lowered recidivism and is, therefore, a cost-efficient use of tax dollars: it is cheaper to educate than to incarcerate. But are prisoners deserving of higher education? Should their education be funded by tax dollars or by the prisoners themselves…or some other way? Should all prisoners have this opportunity, including lifers?

5. A teacher's ultimate accomplishment is when his or her student becomes a teacher, passing on the lessons learned. What lessons did Larry learn from Dr. Bates? Do you think he was a good teacher in prison—and do you believe he would be a good teacher in society if given the chance?

6. Would most husbands be as supportive of their wife's prison work as Allan was? Why or why not? Would you support such work done by your own spouse?

7. In what ways was Dr. Bates's work with prisoners grounded in her parents' experiences as war refugees and immigrants? Do you think, as she does, that they would have approved of her work? Why or why not? Was she right to keep it a secret from them?

8. Both Larry and Dr. Bates accepted a number of challenges in their work. What are some of these challenges—and how did they face them?

9. "This prison doesn't matter," says Larry, referring to the prison of concrete and steel. Breaking out of habitual patterns of self-destructive thinking can be more damaging and more difficult to break out of. How did Larry break those chains, with the help of Shakespeare?

10. Larry feels that we create our own personal prisons, and the author has identified a few of hers throughout the book. Do you feel that they both successfully overcame their own prisons?

11. Every one of the prisoners in the Shakespeare group said he wanted to make a positive contribution to society despite his transgressions. What kinds of contributions are prisoners uniquely able to provide?

12. Macbeth said that he dared not to look on it (his murder) again, but Larry did. The book states that getting convicted killers to look on their crime (i.e., to examine the reasons for the offense) is a key to keeping them from killing again. Why do you think that is so important?

13. Acknowledging responsibility for his crime—as Larry has done—is considered to be an essential ingredient for demonstrating rehabilitation. Why do you think that is so?

14. Look at the following three chapters and consider how you would have reacted.
    Chapter 6—Newton's In
    Chapter 25—The Shower (Me)
    Chapter 26—All Hands on Deck

15. Think about the Shakespeare plays you have read (or read a new one), and consider the ways in which you can find personal relevance in the four-hundred-year-old text. Do one, or more, of the characters have any traits you have? Does he or she face a challenge you have faced? Are there relationships among two or more of the characters that are similar in some ways to your own relationships?

16. What are your own personal prisons—and how can you overcome them?

Acknowledgments

Thanks to literary agent Sandra Choron for the invitation to write this book, and to Shana Drehs and Deirdre Burgess for their expert editorial guidance.

Early drafts of this manuscript benefitted from the careful reading and editorial assistance of Sandra Grasis, Perle Raidonis, Mark Sodetz, Clinton Jackson, Joshua Akens, Andrew Collins, Amber Jones, Daynell Featherstone, and Ruth Fuller.

With the exception of Larry Newton and David Bevington, all other names in this book have been changed.

Some material and some photos were previously published in *Performing New Lives* (Jessica Kingsley Publishers, 2011).

Special thanks to Wabash Valley Correctional Facility for permission to record conversations with prisoners in the Shakespeare Program. And to Larry Newton for sharing his story and for showing that Shakespeare really can save lives.

Most especially to Allan, my partner in crime and everything else for the past thirty years.

About the Author

Dr. Laura Bates is an English professor at Indiana State University, where she has taught courses on Shakespeare for the past fifteen years to students on campus and in prison. She has a PhD from the University of Chicago with a focus on Shakespeare studies. Her work has been featured in national media, including MSNBC's *Lockup*. She lives in Indiana.

Dear Reader:

If you're interested in learning more about the works of William Shakespeare, I invite you to discover the Shakesperience, a hands-on experience with Shakespeare now available on the iBookstore. My publisher, Sourcebooks, created these multimedia, enhanced ebooks in order to help readers overcome some of the challenges presented by the language of the day and to more quickly get to the heart of these life-changing works.

www.sourcebooks.com/shakesperience

Sincerely,
Laura Bates